A
Fifty Years Caring for Animals

By Joseph Priest, DVM

For Dee

Prologue

One last x-ray on Blue, a seven-year-old beagle, would make certain we had gotten all the bladder stones removed. Bladder stones are not uncommon, and can be removed effectively with surgery. The incision through his abdomen was about five inches long. Before closing up his incision, I used clamps to keep the surgery area closed while I quickly wheeled him back to the x-ray. The radiograph would confirm that all the stones were found and removed. Fortunately, I had gotten them all according to the film. In less than five minutes I had him back on the surgery table to suture up the incision and complete the surgery. I put on a new pair of gloves, and then removed the three clamps that held the skin of the incision together. The clamps came off, but the skin stayed put. To my confusion and amazement, the incision did not open. I still needed to suture the inside layers of the surgery, but the skin was staying shut. While I gently pulled it apart, I noticed that it was as if the skin had been lightly glued together. It was a miracle in my mind. The clamps had been on the skin for less than five minutes, and yet the skin had already begun to heal itself.

That was over 40 years ago and I still marvel at how living things heal every time. In every living creature, all the ingredients to grow, survive, heal and thrive are present in every tiny cell. Each cell has its function, and works to reproduce and build and heal, every time, even with no help from humans and technology. It has been an honor to be present to help some animals along in this healing process, but the real marvel is the design of our creation and its amazing ability to beget more life.

It all begins

It was March of 1968 and it was my first day as a veterinarian. I'd been working in a small Plant City, Florida animal hospital less than an hour. It had started off fairly routinely with a slow but steady flow of clients and their pets, mostly visiting for shots and general treatment. I opened the door of a small countertop refrigerator to grab a dose of vaccine and a surprise met my eyes. Inside, filling the entire refrigerator, was a plastic sheet wrapped around a deep brown object. My eyes focused on the long object inside and discerned the form of a horse's head. My life had taken a new turn, everything was going to be differe Born and raised in Tampa, Florida, my family lived on five acres at the northern edge of town in what was then the country. It was a modest, white clapboard home with metal roof shingles that made a wonderful sound when it rained. There was a small barn and a wooden pen which were eventually home to two hereford cows, several chickens and a rabbit. I loved raising farm animals. My father had died when I was 4 years old, and I was the youngest, with two brothers and a sister who were much older. My mother worked hard as a secretary at Tampa Electric Company to keep us all fed, so I was frequently home alone.

The land in Florida is mostly sand, small scrub oaks, palmettos and sandspurs that grow like crazy. Palmettos, which look like miniature palm trees, grow low to the ground with lots of roots and spread everywhere. Snakes, particularly rattlesnakes, are fond of making palmettos their home. Sandspurs, a small weed with many brush-like thorns, are something else. As a boy I hardly ever wore shoes and these sandspurs would definitely get your attention when you stepped on them. My buddies and I would pick them to throw at each other and when they hit your back they stuck and stung. This was the country I grew up in and the place where I dreamed of my future.

My father had grown up on a farm in Tennessee. He kept pigs, cows, chickens and more on our Florida property before he died. My working mother and my busy siblings weren't interested in caring for these creatures, so they were gone when I was very young. As long as I can remember I had been doing odd jobs to earn money. I worked at Lambert's Grocery during the summer stocking shelves for a dollar a day. I was amazed that the cashier made five dollars a day and that the butcher made ten dollars a day. I was about twelve years old when I began mowing grass for Mr. Gant and his yard business. The mowers at this time were not self-propelled and it was tough work to push it. He actually fired me not long after starting for not mowing fast enough. I made up my mind that I would get my job back with this miserly Florida cracker. A few weeks later, I went back to his door to find a wrinkled, frowning face, then asked him to give me another shot. He agreed, and this time I resolved to run with the mower, and I did. His grandson, who also cut grass with us, followed my lead and we often raced one another as we mowed. I was now making that prized $5 a day for my labor. It was not long before I began to accumulate some money. In my room I set up my own small savings plan. I had labeled envelopes in the cubbies atop my dresser which helped me save. One envelope said "cow," while another said "chicken," and another read "rabbit." I had always been interested in farming and this was my first ambition.

I guess I had followed in my father's footsteps even though I never knew him. I began going to local 4-H meetings with a friend whose family had a dairy farm. 4-H is an organization that started more than 100 years ago as a way to bring new farming concepts to younger generations. At the time of the club's conception, older farmers were not receptive to newer farming techniques. Each club member was encouraged to have a project such as rabbit care, cattle raising, quilt-making and more.

My first 4-H project was a Hereford steer named Alex that I raised in the small barn and pasture. Herefords are a breed of cattle that have a white face and a red body. I purchased this steer from another farm and he had a gentle disposition that made him easy to train and handle. He was my pride and joy and I brushed him and walked him on a halter every day. Part of our 4-H program was to show our steers at the state fair in February.

At the fair the smell of cows and hay is wonderful, there was nothing like it. The fairgrounds were always alive with the rumble of trucks delivering animals, the smell of corn dogs and hearty slaps on the backs of my buddies in their matching blue corduroy jackets.

As a sophomore in high school I was competing at the fair, the barn was almost full as I walked down between the two rows of cows facing away from me. Their back ends were facing my way so all that we could see were their long bushy tails swishing back and forth. I worked at the state fair with my classmates, sleeping beside Alex in the hay. There was nothing like laying in the soft bedding, listening to the grunts and rumblings of animals and the giggles and horseplay of old and new friends. No pay, just the fun of missing school two days and helping clean the cow stalls.

One vivid memory I have of that time was set out in back of the fair's barn. The steers that were to be judged were tied to the chain link fence in back to be groomed for the show. By the fence, a 900-pound black Angus steer was nursing on a petite Jersey cow, who couldn't have weighed more than 400 pounds. The steer had been nursing on her since he was born so that he would become the fattest he could be to win the judging contest. She was eating oats in her bucket and he was at her side nursing. He was at least a foot taller than her.

He was almost on his knees to suck a little milk and when it didn't come fast enough from her udder he would bump her from underneath with such force her hind end would come up in the air! It was the strangest site to see this little cow getting bumped up by this huge muscular steer. It looked very uncomfortable to me, but I guess she was used to it. He had nursed on her since he was a young calf. She just kept on munching on her oats.

High school agriculture class stands out in my mind because of one thing — Mr. Hill. Our ag teacher was high strung and excitable, and had a lack of patience that probably wasn't well-suited for teaching a bunch of teenage boys. He tried, oh did he try. A lot of the guys took ag because we didn't have any homework. In our shop we learned how to repair farm machinery, and we had a steel work table and a welding machine. After two pieces of steel were welded together, a layer of slag, or crust, was left on top of the weld. A solid steel chipping hammer was used to knock off the slag when done. Being boys, when Mr. Hill wasn't in the shop, the chipping hammer would somehow get welded to the welding table. This drove Mr. Hill crazy. After this had happened too many times he finally had had enough. His face beet-red, he said, "I want to know who welded the chipping hammer to the table this time?"

No one said a word.

His frustration rising like the mercury in a thermometer, he ordered, "Ok, all you boys go back into the classroom now!" We shuffled slowly out of the shop and took our seats in the adjoining classroom.

His face was now the color of a ripe radish, and he banged his hand on his desk, saying, "I want the person that did this to stand up!"

No one moved.

"Alright, we're going to stay here till I find out who did this."

Again, nothing. His face was getting more flushed and

his frustration increasing. This went on and on. We were trying our best to keep a straight face when he looked our way, and it was very difficult. No one ever stood up.

We sure didn't make his life any easier. Mr. Hill was a really nice guy. One summer he drove me to a summer forestry camp more than 100 miles away and I'll never forget that kindness that he showed to me, despite the antics in shop class.

Blackout

My first experience at a veterinary hospital was just after I had finished high school. Hearing about a job opening at Temple Terrace Animal Hospital, I went to apply. The hospital was a blue concrete block building on a busy street about 12 miles from my home. I had no car at the time, so I pedaled the distance on my second-hand bicycle with no fenders. Fortunately the weather was clear, because when I rode through the mud the missing fenders meant a nice black streak of dirt got flipped up to the middle of my back. After meeting the red-headed receptionist, she took me through the clinic and introduced me to Dr. Robinson. He was about my height and had a ruddy complexion, and I liked him right way. After we had talked for a few minutes he motioned me back and said, "Come on and help me with a surgery, Joe."

I followed him through the many-roomed hospital to the surgery. The room was white with a stainless steel operating table and beige cabinets filled with surgical instruments. As he put on surgical gloves I stared down at a black cat on its belly on the operating table. The endotracheal tube (a clear hollow tube, the size of a pencil, inserted in the windpipe so that the gas anesthesia can be given) stuck out of his mouth. The tube was hooked to a small anesthesia machine and he was sleeping quietly.

He asked me to go to the other side of the table and hold the cat's head so he could operate on his eye.

"This cat has pus inside the eyeball," he stated.

I went to the opposite side of the table and leaned over and placed my arms over the cat, holding my hands on each side of his head. My elbows rested on each side of the cat and my hands cupped on the cat's chin so that Dr. Robinson could operate on the eye. He picked up a scalpel that looked like a dagger about a ½ inch long, and while still talking to me, he pushed the blade directly into the cat's eyeball. The eye deflated like a balloon as pus drained out the bottom of the incision!

At that moment I felt limp and it was as if a black curtain had descended over my brain. Dr. Robinson was still talking to me. If my elbows had not been so firmly set on the table I would have dropped to the floor. In just a few moments the black curtain lifted and I recovered and began to return to the conversation with him. I don't think he ever knew that I passed out because I didn't drop to the floor!

I was not used to pus, surgery and blood. Now, many years later I could eat a baloney sandwich while watching surgery.

Developing a sheet of cardboard

While working at Dr. Robinson's hospital, I wanted to be the best veterinary assistant possible. After x-raying the leg of a very fat English bulldog, Dr. Robinson asked, "Joe would you develop this x-ray for me? The darkroom is over there and we develop in the dark, with no safe light because it's a lot quicker."

He handed me the cassette, a metal plate the size and shape of a legal size folder one half inch thick that held the x-ray film inside. Having worked as a veterinary assistant only two days and having never done this before, I must have had that question mark look on my face. He said, "Once you're in the darkroom and the door is tightly shut, just open the cassette, take out the film, and place it down in the developer fluid tank for three minutes. Then come out with the film."

"Oh, and by the way," he added, "while you're in the dark waiting for the film to develop, reload the cassette with another film."

I must have given him that perplexed look again so he continued, "To load the cassette, just feel around for the box of film below the cabinet, open the top, take out a sheet of film and put it inside the cassette. Then close and lock it."

I marched over to the darkroom to begin developing as instructed. I found out that it's not called it a *darkroom* for nothing! The room was just big enough to stand and so dark I couldn't see my hands when the door was shut. A small table on one wall held the two developing tanks.

Opening the cassette and removing the film, I placed it in the developer solution. I was starting to feel good here, things were going okay. The cassette was open and empty, and getting the new sheet of x-ray film from the box below the tanks was more difficult than I anticipated. The box held 100 sheets of tightly packed film and trying to get one sheet out in total darkness, wasn't easy. Somehow I did it. I closed and locked the cassette and came out with the newly developed film and the freshly loaded cassette. I handed them to Dr. Robinson and was a bit proud of myself.

Dr. Robinson looked at the film.

He said, "Joe, I need one more."

Dr. Robinson took another x-ray, then handed me another cassette to be developed.

"No problem," I replied, certain that I was now an experienced x-ray developer. Back in the darkroom, I followed the same procedure as before, noticing the film didn't feel quite the same in the pitch dark as the first one. Of course I couldn't see anything, but this sheet of film that I put in the developing tank was not as smooth and felt a little thicker, as if it had been sanded to a rougher finish.

Returning from the darkroom and bringing the second film to him he held it up to the light. After he had looked at the film a few moments a slow smile began at the corners of his mouth and soon spread to a full grin. "Joe, I think you have developed a sheet of cardboard."

The film didn't look like an X-ray but had a brownish clay color that you couldn't see through at all like the first film. I would have liked to have gone back to the darkroom and disappeared. He patiently explained to me that a box of x-ray film is packed very tightly with 100 sheets. Three or four cardboard spacers are put in between the sheets to keep them from sticking together and I had unknowingly selected the cardboard spacer instead of the film.

Well, so much for being the *best* veterinary assistant!

University of South Florida, 1960

My hometown had been growing during my high school years, and a brand new university was opening in Tampa. I enrolled at the University of South Florida in the fall of 1960 with about 800 other students. We were the meager first class of a university which now boasts 48,000 students. I lived at home and paid my own tuition with my savings from the lawn business and my part-time work at the animal clinic. At that time, tuition was about $90 a semester, which seems hard to believe now. I would hitch a ride with friends to the campus, where I studied pre-veterinary medicine. I had never been a serious student, but I knew I wanted to become a veterinarian. I had to learn to apply myself in a whole new way to survive these classes. I took a quick course that helped me learn to memorize large quantities of information quickly. This would be crucial as my studies progressed.

One class gave me an entirely new education that I wasn't expecting. American History with Dr. Rubin was on my schedule as a freshman. I hated this professor. He had an abrupt, in-your-face demeanor and was a Yankee from New York City. We Southerners distrusted Yankees. I grew up in a segregated school, a segregated city, a segregated state and a segregated South, and I knew nothing else than this way of life. I didn't dislike non-white persons and never really thought about how it might have been different or wrong for persons of color to have to sit at the balcony of the theatre or use a different bathroom. I always just accepted this situation as the way things were. This was a turbulent time in history and the civil rights movement was growing. As a young, ignorant Southern man, I thought (without much thought), "Why can't they just stay in their place?" This was the accepted thinking of my friends, family and everyone I knew at the time.

Dr. Rubin hammered on the injustice of this system during the history class. Every Tuesday and Thursday for an hour and a half I heard the same message over and over and over again. He would ask in every single class, "What if you were born black?"

My first reaction was that I wasn't born black, so what difference does it make? I wondered why he just wouldn't get on with the course. At some point later in the course I actually gave that question a thought and began to seriously ponder what life would be like if I had been born black. The more I thought about it, I began to feel rage when imagining my own reaction to being asked to sit only in the balcony to watch a movie, or to have to order and receive my meal from a restaurant back window rather than being permitted to sit inside at a table.

    Slowly and steadily my perspective started to change. I began to accept each person by his or her name, rather than referring to them by the color of their skin or their ethnicity. It took time over the course of my life, but I learned to make genuine friendships with non-white persons and I now see the world in a different light. The injustice of segregation can never be overlooked by me again. The discomfort and frustration that I felt with Dr. Rubin sparked a meaningful and important change in me, and to this day I am grateful that he was there at that point in my life.

    After two years of basic courses at USF, I needed a certain number of agriculture courses to be accepted at veterinary school. USF did not offer the ag classes I needed, so it was time to venture away from home for the first time in my life. The University of Florida, 120 miles north of Tampa, offered the classes I needed and I headed to Gainesville in the fall of 1962. I found a room to rent in a house six miles from campus. My friend Lawrence Fitzgerald had moved to Gainesville a few years earlier as a researcher, and the home he shared with his mother provided me economical and ideal room and board. Lawrence was confined to a wheelchair and had a PhD in mathematics. He was doing research on the first CT scan machines. He was a genius. His mother Mrs. Fitzgerald was an excellent cook, and while I biked 12 miles a day to and from campus, I devoured her hearty southern meals with gusto and never had to watch my weight.

At that time there was no veterinary school in Florida and Auburn University in Alabama was the closest college to study animal medicine. Auburn accepted only 20 new students from the state of Florida each fall, and more than 400 students applied, making the competition stiff. Auburn accepted many more in-state students than out-of-state. The population of Alabama was about 2 million at the time, and the university accepted about 60 of their local students.

I had several close friends who also had their sights on veterinary school like me. Ed, Gene, Alan and myself would meet at the Hub student center at Florida and often had scant change in our pockets. We would even pool together our coins to buy one donut and split it for breakfast. Jean had been a jockey before heading to UF, but had then grown too tall to continue in horse racing. We would abscond newspapers from nearby tables at the Hub and Jean would pick the winners for the horse races that day. Wow, could he pick 'em! If we could have bet, we would have won a lot of money. We all felt the pressure to get accepted to veterinary school and grades were crucial to the process. It seemed the agriculture professors were out for blood against pre-vet students.

After two years of qualification courses in agriculture, the four of us applied to Auburn, and to our great dismay, we were all turned down. We could apply next year, but all our required courses were done. A bachelor's degree was not required to apply for vet school. We were at a crossroads as to whether to go on with studies at UF and earn a degree in agriculture, which offered few employment prospects, or to try applying again. Jean, Alan and Ed made the decision to stick with their UF studies and earn a BS in agriculture. I had a different idea. I would move to Alabama, work for a year, and then reapply for Auburn's vet school the following fall. To be considered an Alabama student, I had to show proof of residence and employment in the state for 12 months.

After a short trip home to say goodbye to my mother, I packed my duffel bag and asked my mother to drive me to the highway to head north. In the early 1960s hitchhiking was common, cheap and faster than the bus. I hitched a ride to Prattville, Alabama, a tiny village outside Montgomery, where a friend had helped me find a job at a cotton gin factory. I had never seen a cotton gin in my life.

I rented a room in a house which belonged to my friend's brother. I had never been to Alabama and the hills and kudzu growing everywhere sure looked different than Florida. My job at the cotton gin factory was to keep track of the time spent on all the various tasks that comprised building the cotton gin machines. My pay was $25 per week, which didn't go far. I soon moved to a small apartment in Montgomery, 14 miles away, and rode to and from work with other gin factory co-workers. I joined a Baptist church and got involved in a social group there, but it was still a lonely time. My 21st birthday came in October and I visited a bar alone, eager to order my first beer. It was quite a letdown when the bartender did not even ask for my ID.

The cotton gin factory was a large metal building about the size of two football fields, and it was the assembly area for the cotton gin machines which were shipped all over the world. A cotton gin looks like a giant piano that Gulliver might have used in the land of Lilliput. They are about seven feet high and 12 feet wide with a shaft full of circular sawblades instead of a row of keys. Those sawblades spun quickly to remove the seeds from the harvested cotton balls, but I never got to see these monstrous machines in action.

As timekeeper, I had plenty of time to talk to the guys

on the assembly line. They were mostly much older than me, with thick Southern accents and wearing weathered bib overalls. These guys would spend a lot of time talking about foxhunting and their dogs on Monday mornings. After weeks of working and listening to these conversations, I had to ask one of the guys about foxhunting.

"Henry, what is foxhunting? Do you really catch a fox and eat it?" I inquired.

"Nah. We go out in the woods on Saturday night and let the dogs loose. We build a big fire to sit around, drink whiskey and listen to the dogs baying and tell lies," he said.

Then the men went home to bed, only to return to the woods in the morning and pick up their dogs.

During a mild day in November I was across the street from the factory at a lunch counter when I heard the news that President Kennedy had been shot. I was stunned and deeply saddened. I had really admired him and was inspired by his *"Ask not what your country can do for you, ask what you can do for your country"* message. I was disappointed and dismayed when I returned to work and heard my work friends saying, "Good. I'm glad they shot him."

It was clear proof to me that the civil rights movement had a long way to go.

Auburn University, 1964

Being accepted to veterinary school was one of the high points of my life. After 3-4 years of college you can apply to veterinary school along with a whole lot of other candidates. The four months waiting to hear if you have been accepted is tense. The day the envelope arrived I didn't want to open it right away, thinking if I waited a little bit that the news might be better. After a long wait, I finally relented. On opening it, I found a form letter.

```
We wish to inform you
```
Joseph Priest

☑ ```You have been accepted to the Auburn University Veterinary School```

☐ ```You have not been accepted to the Auburn University Veterinary School```

The line that said *"You have been accepted…"* was checked. That was as far as I got before I jumped and yelled. I immediately went to the pay phone and called my mother to share the good news. She was very excited. I then gave my notice to my employers at the cotton gin factory and moved to the "Loveliest Village on the Plains," Auburn, Alabama. I had visited this small, sleepy town in eastern Alabama during my time working in Prattville. I felt at ease and at home in this college village with aged brick buildings and oak-lined streets. As a visitor walking down Main Street (or nearly any street) in tiny Auburn, nearly every passerby greeted me with a smile and a warm "hello" or "hey." Also, I was delighted to see the abundance of rah-rah shoes on the feet of many students. Even though these classic two-color lace-up loafers have come to be a symbol of the generation, I had rarely seen them during my time at USF and UF. I had a small rented room on the second floor of a brick house on Magnolia, at Little Henry's Boarding House. As I recall my room and board was about $8 a week, which included an abundant bounty of hearty, Southern food served family style. I started classes in the summer of 1964.

As I was paying my own way, I needed a job, and the lake at Chewacla State Park outside Auburn needed a lifeguard. I worked two or three days a week when I didn't have class. Chewacla was a beautiful lake that was quiet on weekdays, and busy on the weekends. I had a dark blue 1950 Studebaker by this point that I had bought in Prattville for $25. It had been sitting in a co-worker's front yard for about four years. Low gear was stripped out, and the battery had died years ago. However, I always tried to park it on a hill facing downward, so that all I had to do was release the brake, let it roll and let the clutch out and it would start in second gear. This got me around short distances, but I would borrow a friend's car for a date, and hitchhike when I needed to get back to Tampa.

Lifeguarding is a pretty boring job the vast majority of the time. One Sunday afternoon I sat in my chair and watched a boy, about eight years old, swimming with his father out towards a raft in the center of the lake. As I watched he began to fall behind his father. His swimming stroke started to become erratic, and I sat up a little taller and squinted. It was clear he was struggling, and no longer going forward in the water. His head began to bob under and above the water. I jumped down off the lifeguard chair and dove in the water from the beach. I swam out to him as quickly as I could and hooked my arm around his waist. As the raft was closer than the beach, I swam him up to the raft to reunite him with his father. As I returned to my lifeguard chair I began to think about how quickly the life of a healthy child could end. It was an eye-opener, and as I look back, it helped continue to form my marvel and fascination with the way in which life sustains and restores itself. In one moment the boy is flailing and near death, and minutes later he is strong and renewed with fresh air in his lungs on the raft.

Alpha Psi

Around the Auburn campus I began to meet some of the vet students. It wasn't long before they began to tell me about Alpha Psi, the professional fraternity for veterinary students. The guys had just built a house on the northern area of the campus, close to the vet school buildings, and needed vet students to move in. It seemed like a good arrangement, so I packed my only duffle bag and moved to the end room by a little creek. It was a sparsely furnished single-story house with a plain cement floor and space for about 35 guys and a house mother.

Every fraternity at Auburn was required to have a house mother at the time. Our Alpha Psi house mother was a tiny, elderly, blue-haired, blue-blooded Alabama matron who was called Miss Kate. She had a heavy Southern drawl and was much troubled by the lack of thoroughness on behalf of the house employees, who were all African-Americans. She called them "the servants," and was often on the frat president's case to hound the three unfortunate employees to be attentive to her needs.

"Henry, you need to tell these servants to keep this floor swept every day," she would say in her syrupy Southern accent. Her Old South attitude toward "the help" both frustrated and tickled the Florida guys like me who were not accustomed to servants of any kind. She might have seemed cultured and old-fashioned, but those of us from Florida and other states besides the Deep South recognized her demeanor was troubling. She was a product of her time, but at this point in my education I could see the prejudice.

The house shared a great collegiality. Sunday through Thursday we studied, and Fridays and Saturdays we partied. Collectively we shared a sentiment of "cooperate and graduate." Although we enjoyed ourselves, we all felt the pressure to pass all of our courses. In vet school, failing to pass any course meant being kicked out of the school, and then all of the previous work goes down the drain. One of my classmates who was already married, found a clever but helpful way to aid our success. Rusty Taylor would take meticulous notes during our classes, then give them to his wife, who would type them and make copies for all of us. The rest of our classmates would all chip in to pay her for her efforts, which helped us all to study and gave them extra income.

One of our vet school courses was Poisonous Plants, as cows, horses and other animals occasionally eat toxic plants, and it was our job to recognize which plants were harmful as we learned how to treat this poisoning. Part of the course entailed collecting samples of various poisonous plants and turning in a dried plant portfolio. Upperclassmen at our Alpha Psi house were helpful in knowing good spots to look for these plants, as they had already scouted out surrounding fields and pastures. Also, if one of us in the class was fortunate enough to find some crotalaria weed, an oleander bush or a buckeye tree, we would take a good many samples to share with our fellow classmates, who were already on the hunt for other poison plants to share.

    I had half-heartedly joined a fraternity as an undergrad at the University of Florida, but my experience with Alpha Psi was nothing like the hazing and stupid pranks that I experienced while at UF. The camaraderie and fellowship of my vet school buddies from the Alpha Psi house continues to this day. We have reunions and gatherings that rekindle our college days, even continuing to help one another—although now it is mostly in finding good seats for Auburn football games.

    I remember my classmate Jerry Reed did not buy a medical dictionary as was recommended for our classes. We used to tease Jerry that he wasn't going to graduate if he didn't have one. Thirty years later I texted Jerry, who had a practice 40 minutes north of my clinic.

I said to him, "Jerry, the Dean found out that you didn't have a medical dictionary and he wants you to return your diploma."

He texted me back a picture of himself sitting with his feet up on his desk holding a medical dictionary. The text said, "I borrowed this one today and tell him I'm not sending my diploma in."

PT Climbs in Window

The histology laboratory was on the first floor of the physiology building. It was a stark, square two-story brick building in which we spent countless hours studying the way body systems work together, and how body tissues are made. Heads craned over microscopes, we studied things like urinary bladders and how the cells of these tissues stretch and contract when needed. Dr. Wittson was our histology professor and it was late in the school term. We were young, it was spring time, and our attention was not always focused. Dr. Wittson was blind in one eye and he had to turn his head to one side to read his lecture notes. He was high strung and uneasy, with receding black hair and thick glasses. The lectures lasted two hours with a 15-minute break in the middle. After the break some students were frequently late to return to class and this irritated Dr. Wittson greatly.

One day he made an announcement at the beginning of class, "Mrs. Dansen, please close and lock the doors at the end of the break."

Mrs. Dansen, a quiet, friendly and unassuming lab assistant, was about as opposite from Dr. Wittson as could be. On this day, she was dressed in a pale green plaid dress and she sat at the back of the class by the door. She acknowledged his instructions with a nod of her head.

Our break came and it looked like everyone made it back in. Mrs. Dansen locked the door as instructed. All was quiet as Dr. Wittson resumed lecturing, head cocked to one side to read his lecture notes, as Mrs. Dansen sat in the back by the locked door. We heard a knock on the door. No one said a word—all eyes remained on the professor.

Again came a knock, louder this time.

All of us knew it was P.T., a classmate from Mississippi, outside the door, and he hadn't made it in on time. He was tough and swarthy and we all knew him only by his initials.

No one moved and Dr. Wittson continued to lecture. He was now talking louder to overcome the banging on the door. Mrs. Dansen kept her seat by the door and tension began to rise. The knocks continued, more like banging now, and Dr. Wittson continued to lecture and ignore the knocking. Mrs. Dansen, holding her seat by the door, did a great job of trying to ignore the knocking and follow our professor's instructions. We students were glued to our seats and tried our best to stifle any laughs, not knowing what would happen next. One more time *a banging on the door* came so loudly that we thought the doors were going to come off their hinges! We all sat quietly, as Mrs. Dansen looked straight ahead, her hands folded primly on her lap, not leaving her seat as instructed. The tension was rising to a fever pitch.

Then there was quiet for a few minutes and we thought P.T. had given up. I was slowly beginning to concentrate on the lesson once again. A few minutes later, out of the corner of my eyes, I could see P.T. climbing in the window a few feet from Mrs. Dansen! It was May in Alabama, and our vet school had no air conditioning anywhere. The roll out windows were open full-tilt, leaving two-foot openings right along the lab countertops. Everyone in the class could see P.T. slowly climbing through the opening from the outside, and we tried our best not to startle or laugh.

Dr. Wittson could not see P.T. at the window, as he had his head bent over his lecture notes in a way that allowed him to see with his good eye. Mrs. Dansen, although she could see P.T., kept her eyes glued to the front. Presumably she did not want to upset Dr. Wittson.

Just as P.T. had gotten one leg over the window ledge and onto the laboratory counter, Dr. Wittson looked up, turned his head to one side to see with his good eye, and saw P.T. His face slowly changed to crimson like mercury rising in a thermometer. He threw the chalk in his hand down on the counter breaking it into several pieces and stormed out of the room. P.T. continued on over the lab counter and took his seat as if nothing had happened.

There was dead silence in the classroom, and no one knew what would happen next. We were freshmen and deathly afraid of flunking out (after working hard for 3 to 4 years of college to be admitted to veterinary school we didn't want to forsake that by flunking out now). I think we were all thinking that this would be it for P.T.!

After a few minutes Dr. Wittson came back in. His face was now a little less flushed, and he resumed his lecture as if nothing had happened. He must have had a talk with himself in the office, but P.T. did not flunk out.

First Hog Farm Visit

I spent a good part of my childhood raising cows, horses and other farm animals, but I had never kept hogs. One of our clinical rotations was large animal ambulatory--our veterinary version of an ambulance was an extended-cab pick-up truck. It seated six students and one professor, who drove us to our farm visit. It was a tight fit in that pick-up. Our first visit was to a small farm just outside of Auburn. It was a simple white-clapboard farmhouse with a wisteria vine growing over one side. The hog pen sat behind the house, out of immediate sight. As I opened the truck door, the stifling stench of 40 full-grown hogs assaulted my nose, but that wasn't going to be the worst part. The professor instructed us to put on our rubber boots, which were a part of the books and supplies that vet students had to buy or acquire. I hadn't really thought about why we needed the boots until this moment.

We walked out to a pig pen behind the house and found a 50 feet by 50 feet sty. A four-foot wooden fence surrounded a huge pit of black, well-churned muck. The hogs wallowed about, up to their bellies in wretched feces and mud. Although the phrase "happy as a pig in mud" is somewhat true, pigs do benefit from more space and a somewhat cleaner area. However, pig farming, and most other livestock farming, has routinely limited animals to smaller spaces for convenience in caring for the animals. This particular sty was knee-deep in excrement and putrid mud. The odor was enough to floor you!

We gathered our equipment from the back of the truck. Each of us had a syringe and a bottle of vaccine. We marched over to the hogs, ready for duty.

Our professor, Dr. Newman, said, "Get in there, boys, and vaccinate the hogs."

I climbed over the fence and down into the thick black mud. It was deeper than it looked. The mud oozed over the top of my boots and down into my feet before I even took a step. We gave the hogs their vaccine without too much trouble, chasing them down one at a time, because the thick mud slowed them down. As we vaccinated each hog, we shooed him over to other side of the fence to keep the vaccinated ones separate from the pigs who still needed a shot. After a half-hour, we finished and headed back to the truck. Jerry, my lab partner, elbowed me in the ribs, laughing as he said, "Joe, you stink!" We all did, it was one smelly ride back.

Bullethead

Dr. Neal taught us microbiology--the study of microscopic organisms such as bacteria, protozoa and fungi. He was a retired army officer who did not originate from the South. His head was completely bald and he was rather portly. Despite his stern ex-military presence, he was kind-hearted and helpful in the difficult task of identifying different species of bacteria under a microscope.

Lester Spell from Mississippi had the longest, slowest southern drawl I've ever heard, and I had heard quite a few accents by this point in my education. We were in the last few weeks of the spring quarter and feeling like the summer break couldn't arrive soon enough. Feeling a little bold outside of the classroom, a few of the guys began referring to Dr. Neal as "Bullethead." In his white lab coat with his bald head and rotund body, he did indeed look something like a bullet standing on end.

On a hot Wednesday afternoon, we sat at the lab counter looking into our microscopes. Lester was across from me examining his slides. Looking a bit like Alfred Hitchcock with his portly stomach, Dr. Neal was walking around behind us with hands in his lab coat pockets. He roamed about answering student questions.

Lester had his head down concentrating on the view in his microscope, and said to his lab partner Hugh, in his characteristic drawl, "Hugh, tell ole Bullethead to come over here and look at this slide."

What Lester didn't know was that "ole Bullethead" was standing right behind him!

No one said a word. Dr. Neal just kept on walking as if he didn't hear what Lester said. We just knew Lester was a goner. We were certain that all that effort to gain admission to veterinary school was down the tubes for him. Failing one class meant veterinary school was over, and there were few multiple choice tests in vet school. Each course meant that your grades were determined solely by your professor's individual evaluation of your work.

Lester graduated with us and, as far as I know, nothing ever came of this.

The Army Calls

During my time at Auburn, I had been called for a physical exam for the draft. All men 18 to 25 years old had to register for the draft and when called for the physical, had to report to the requesting location. For me, I had to go to a military base outside of Montgomery, Alabama. A bus was provided to get you there, and it was mandatory and there was no rescheduling this event.

We were told to bring a toothbrush with us as the exam might take more than a day. I wasn't really sure how long it would take to get a physical and be evaluated for military service, but other men were saying that there would be no coming back. Many men said we would go straight from the physical to Vietnam and would not see our families again before leaving. It did not turn out to be true, but it was an anxiety-filled and scary time nonetheless.

The physical took several days. It consisted of walking around in your underwear with about 500 other guys and going from station to station. We carried a folder with all of our documents that was completed at each station--the eye exam, ear exam and so forth. I particularly remember the blood-drawing station. All of us guys were in line to have our blood drawn, and the medic performing the draws was having no problem.

When I finally got to the front of the line, the medic stood up and said, "Okay, Henry, you try it now."

The medic beside him was clearly holding the syringe for the first time. I don't remember how many times he poked around in my arm and rooted for a vein, but it sure did hurt. Most of our day was spent sitting in a folding chair and awaiting instructions as to which station to go to next. After two days of medical exams and sleeping in barracks, one of the guys decided to approach the sergeant sitting at a desk at the front of the hangar.

"Excuse me, when do we go home?" he asked.

The sergeant stood up with an ugly look on his face and said, "Sit down! I'll tell you when to get up!"

The next day, with relief, we were loaded back on the buses and returned home.

When's he gonna wake up, Doc?

Dr. Wiggins was one of the friendliest, soft-spoken and best professors that we had. He seemed to know us all by name, and was more approachable than many of the other professors. We loaded up in the school truck to go on a farm call in Loachapoka, about 15 miles from the school. After arriving, the old farmer in bib overalls walked us over to a very sick mule. Grey in color, with huge ears like all mules have, he had a blank look as he hung his head down almost to the ground. Dr. Wiggins examined him while the farmer, chewing his tobacco, held the mule's head.

When he had finished, Dr. Wiggins said to him, "He's very old and sick and I'm afraid there is nothing more we can do for him. We will have to put him to sleep, and then we'll take him back to the veterinary college for an autopsy."

The farmer nodded his agreement.

Dr. Wiggins pulled up the euthanasia solution in a large syringe, and then gave the injection to put the mule to sleep. The old mule slowly sank to the ground, as the pentobarbital works very quickly and painlessly. We loaded his body in the back of the truck. As we drove back to the college with the dead mule in the back of our truck, the farmer followed us in his pickup truck.

At the college we backed the truck up to the autopsy floor and began to unload his body. The farmer stood beside Dr. Wiggins as we worked.

He asked Dr. Wiggins, "When's he gonna wake up, doc?"

Dr. Wiggins gently explained to him, "He's not going to wake up. *Put to sleep* means to put to sleep forever."

He was fine with this explanation, and understood it had to be done because he knew there was no more treatment we could do for him.

Many times in our profession the term *put to sleep* is used day in and day out in the hospital and we forget how it might be misunderstood. For instance in a hospital we say *put him down* or *put him to sleep,* and it means to give the animal anesthesia before performing surgery. If an animal was brought into the hospital because he was very sick, suffering and no more treatment was possible, we might point to his cage and say the exact same words. We are going to *put him down* or *put him to sleep* means that he will be euthanized or put to sleep forever. These are the same words but have a completely different meaning in different contexts.

Looking back, it's a wonder there isn't more confusion with this term.

Dr. Fitzgerald

I'm sure that Dr. Fitzgerald, our histology professor, was a very good professor in his day. He even wrote the book for our course. It just so happened that we had his class in his last year of teaching, while he was in his late seventies.

We were sophomores, it was spring, the last quarter before summer break and classes were, to say the least, getting monotonous. Dr. Fitzgerald had thick grey hair, wore wire rim glasses and was slight in stature. He always wore a coat and tie to class. Ties were mandatory in vet school for all of the male students at the time. Ladies, of which there were two in my vet class of 100, wore dresses and heels.

He must have had false teeth that were loose or some other problem with his mouth or teeth, because the way he talked he sounded as if he had rocks in his mouth. We referred to him as "mangle mouth." When he said something like simple squamous epithelium, it came out like schimle schamus espithelum.

This was the early 1960's and the hearing aid that he wore was the size of a pocket radio. He kept in his inside coat pocket with a wire connected to his hearing aid that led up to a plug in his ear.

As Dr. Fitzgerald lectured about tissues and their

importance, we couldn't understand much of what he said. Some of the time one of the guys would stand to ask a question and only 'mouth' the words. Dr. Fitzgerald would then reach into his coat pocket to furiously turn up the hearing aid. I am not proud of this behavior, but we were prone to a few pranks to help get through the tedious and laborious studies.

Despite his age and his speech and hearing problem, Dr. Fitzgerald taught me fascinating things about tissues and their function in living creatures. Through his book (which still remains on my bookcase) and his young colleagues, whom he had mentored at the vet school, Dr. Fitzgerald left his mark upon my veterinary education.

One of the most interesting lessons I remember regarded the cells of the kidney. When food is eaten and digested, it is broken down into its various components-- carbohydrates, protein and fats. These components become fuel for a living being, much like gas fuels a car. When carbohydrates and fat are burned, all that remains is carbon dioxide and water. The proteins, however, are reduced to amino acids after they have been processed for the body's fuel. These amino acids in the blood will become urine. The amino acids are filtered from the blood by the kidney in a small, but crucial, filter called glomeruli. Just as in humans, animals have two kidneys, which contain multitudes of glomeruli. Sorting and passing the amino acids through the glomeruli in the kidneys onto the bladder is a crucial function of every living being. This is one of the few places in the body where a component of the blood is allowed to pass through the wall of the blood vessel into the receptacle for urine, which is the urinary tract.

When the glomeruli are damaged from toxic substances or age, then other non-damaged glomeruli must take their place and work twice as hard. If too many glomeruli are damaged, then urine backs up into the blood stream and jaundice occurs. This is called uremia and death occurs if this is not alleviated. In humans this is what dialysis and kidney transplants treat. Unfortunately this is not a realistic option for most pets, given the tremendous cost and shorter lifespans of most domestic animals.

Understanding these tiny, microscopic cells in the tissue of the kidney was another moment of great fascination for me. Without this tissue performing its job, life cannot be sustained. A body can compensate for much damage to this tissue, and still continue to function. This is true for a great many systems, and pondering this still leaves me marveling at the power of nature to heal and survive.

Asa, call Jimmie

Veterinary school was filled with much studying, much angst, and much camaraderie to let off some steam. Asa was a very smart classmate, one of those lucky guys that didn't have to study like the rest of us. Like so many geniuses, he was easy to trick.

Dr. James Greene was dean of our veterinary school. In the back of our minds, we worried that something bad would happen, such as a disastrous test grade or a major screw-up that would cause us to flunk out and render all the years we had put into professional school for naught. We never wanted to cross a professor. The thought of even talking to the dean was beyond comprehension.

There was only one phone in the veterinary fraternity house where I lived with about 40 other veterinary school students. It was a pay phone, and it was mounted to the wall at the end of the hallway. There were two long rows of hallways with about 10 rooms on each side, and the phone sat at the intersection in the middle. This was the sole phone in the house to call home. We had a blackboard beside it to leave return call messages. There were no answering machines at the time.

Every so often, on the chalkboard, we would leave a message that said "Asa, call Jimmie. 344-2349." This was Dean Greene's home phone number.

Sure enough Asa would see the message and call, saying, "Hello, is Jimmie there?"

We did this over and over before he caught on. What fun we had!

Tugboats

One of the ways I was able to continue paying for college was by working on tug boats. I worked summers and holiday breaks. I enjoyed this work very much.

Tugboat work began when I went to live with my older sister Nancy in the summer in Galliano, the most southern part of Louisiana. My first job was on a tug that worked in the oil fields about 88 miles offshore in the Gulf of Mexico.

The tugs working this far out in the gulf were called sea-going tugs, as opposed to river tugs which are smaller because they don't have to go through the violent storms that occur out at sea. The waves out there can be as high as 25 to 30 feet and even 100 feet if caught in a hurricane, which is exactly what happened to me, as I will explain later.

As I stepped onto my first boat, an older red and white tug named the *Dolores Rogers*, the first mate met me at the rail.

"Hi, I'm Steve. You can put your stuff in there and I'll show you around," he said.

He introduced me to the crew as "Joe," but that's the last time I ever heard my real name used. From then on I was known as "college boy." The crew, this one was from Mississippi, had worked together for twenty-something years and the guys that worked the summers out of college were simply known as college boy. I didn't mind as I saw that's what they called all of the college guys out here.

Our tug boat would bring out supplies to a huge lay barge (the size of a ship) that was welding a pipeline from the many oil rigs out in the gulf back to the shore. Also, the tug repositioned the barge by moving its four large anchors. The lay barge, as it was called, held 250 men that lived and worked there for two weeks at a time working on a three-foot diameter pipeline which was being welded together, section by section, and was laid down on the bottom of the Gulf of Mexico from the well to the refinery on the land.

I was a deckhand, the lowest position on the tug. The *Dolores Rogers*--boats are always named for women as good luck--had a crew of nine men. Four deckhands, a cook, two engineers, the first mate Steve and the captain. The *Dolores Rogers* was not a new boat, and there was a single cabin for sleeping, with only five bunks for sleeping. With nine men on the boat, this meant we had to "hot bunk." Since watches ran 24 hours a day, we took turns sleeping in the bunks.

The normal routine was to work at sea for two weeks and be off one week. As it played out for me, being single at the time, there was usually someone who wanted to be off so I'd take their shift and would end up working the summer straight through. Everything you need is supplied on the boat and the only way to spend any money was to gamble, which didn't interest me, so at the end of the summer I had enough money to pay for my tuition.

One night, after I had been working several weeks on the boat, a diver got on our boat with Lefty, his tender, at three in the morning. Tugboats are manned for 24 hours a day in watches of six hours on and six hours off. My watch was noon to 6 pm and midnight to 6 am, so I was on duty when we pulled up alongside the lay barge and picked up the two men. The large, muscular diver and his small, scrawny tender Lefty got on our boat, and I wondered what was going to happen.

The water was ink black, it was foggy, and a light breeze blew over the boat as it bobbed in five foot swells. Going out about two miles into the empty ocean we stopped, and captain turned on the searchlight above the wheelhouse. It cast a strange glow out on the mist. The diver put on work overalls and a toolbelt, which he loaded with wrenches and a flashlight. Next came the flippers and facemask as he sat on the railing waiting to jump in the water.

I asked Lefty, who tended the air supply hose for the diver, how deep the water was out here. He replied that is was about 250 feet deep. The diver sat on railing for a few minutes and adjusted his facemask. He checked his microphone with Lefty.

Then, over the railing the diver went, and I was aghast. He was going to dive down into the black ocean by himself down to 250 feet! I thought to myself that he would never come back, as there was no telling what could be down there to eat him. I could hear Lefty over the next hour or so talking to the diver as he repaired the pipes down below, so I surmised he was still alive.

As we waited in the ominous mist, I was out on the front deck in a daydream, looking at the foggy sea which was eerily lit by the searchlight. As the waves were gently rolling by, I noticed something in the water at the outer edge of the searchlight's beam. Was it a seagull sitting in the water?

As the waves continued to roll by, the object began to come into view. I walked up to the railing to see what it was. To my astonishment it looked like a hand floating, fingers up! Immediately I thought, oh no!, this is a body and all I could see was a hand. Should I call the captain?

The hand continued to float closer to the boat, and I could finally see that it was only a rubber work glove that had fallen off one of the oil rigs. It certainly got my heart pumping. Meanwhile, the diver was still down below in that murky water. I worried that he might never return, but two hours later there he was, climbing back on the boat. He had been working down at 250 feet for less than one hour but at that depth he had to come back up slowly for what seemed like two more hours to decompress. I was sure glad he made it!

Rudy

The next summer I got a job on a seagoing tug that sailed from Crystal River, Florida, and went across the Gulf of Mexico to New Orleans. This was newer and larger than the previous tugs. My new girlfriend, who will be introduced later, drove me from Tampa up the 40 or so miles to the Crystal River Landing where the boat was docked. I kissed her goodbye and boarded the boat. She was a beautiful boat, named the *Carmen Perez*.

I was introduced all around. Our captain, Jack Revell, was very laid back and friendly. There was the typical crew — captain, first mate, chief engineer, second engineer, four deckhands and Rudy the cook. Our boat towed a large coal barge, the size of a ship, by a steel cable three to four inches in diameter. The barge was attached by a cable about a thousand feet behind the boat. The empty barge was taken on the three-day trip north about 500 miles to New Orleans where it was loaded with coal before heading back to the power plant in Crystal River. The barge was much larger than our tug which pulled it. The tug probably could have fit into one of the four holds on the barge.

During that summer I got to know the crew of the *Carmen Perez* well. Rudy, our cook, was what you would call high-strung. Actually, that might be an understatement. He was very high strung! We all had to come to the galley to eat at the right time, then be out when done so he could clean up. He was a nice guy but always bouncing around like a ping pong ball!

Meals were a big event on all the tugs I worked on, as it was the only real variety to the day. The food was generally very good and highly anticipated throughout the long workdays. Over a meal we could discuss the fine points of most dishes. While our treat for the day was a good meal, Rudy himself enjoyed fishing when he wasn't working in the galley. He seemed to always have a baited line tied off to the bollard—a short post the thickness of a telephone pole where ropes are tethered when docked. His regular routine was to serve our supper, clean away the dishes and go out to the back deck to check his line.

The speed of our tug was about 12 miles an hour under tow. This is a little fast for trolling with a fishing line, so I don't remember Rudy catching too many fish, although he always kept at it. His temperament set him up for a little practical joking. One afternoon the deckhands pulled in his fishing line and tied a 40-pound steel shackle to it and threw it back in the water. That night after we finished supper we all left and went up to the wheelhouse, where we could see the back deck. We waited. After Rudy finished cleaning the dishes, he went to the back deck and checked his fishing line.

This was usually a simple tug of the line while looking out to the water to see if something was there. Now all the deckhands were watching and just about to explode with laughter. He checked his line and it was tighter than a guitar string. You could tell he was excited as he looked around for anyone else on deck. Usually there was always somebody around to share some exciting news, but we were all stashed away in the wheelhouse. Rudy began to pull in the line, which was not easy. It took several minutes. When he pulled up the shackle, he threw it on the deck and you could see the crimson begin to rise in his face. He was madder than a hornet!

Our fun cost us during the next day's meals.

Hurricane

My day began at 2:30 am on September 9, 1965, as I left southern Louisiana for New Orleans. I was heading to the dock to board my tug for the last time before returning to college in the fall. Although Hurricane Betsy was off the coast in Miami more than 900 miles away, and it wasn't known which way it would travel next, I wasn't worried. I would be doing my last trip on a river tug somewhat smaller than the sea-going tug that worked in the New Orleans harbor.

At the landing, the captain, the other deckhand and I loaded our food and other needed supplies onto a crew boat that would take us out to our tug, the *Joe McDermott*. I should have known we were in for some bad luck because this one was not named after a woman.

Well, here we go again, I thought — another seven days on the boat. After we were underway, we tied on to a sand barge and began to tow it up the industrial canal to a landing where we tied it off and left it there. Now a light boat, a tug with nothing in tow, we headed down the canal toward the Mississippi River.

The wind had begun to blow pretty hard while we were moving the barge. Although the *Joe* was a small river tug, 30 to 40 mile per hour winds didn't bother us at all. Earlier that summer I had worked on a seagoing tug and this weather was nothing compared with the 10 to 12 foot waves we had encountered out there. In fact, it felt good to me to feel a boat rock a little. I just didn't know then that I was going to get all the rocking and danger I'd ever want!

About 10:30 am the marine weather reports said that the hurricane was now moving at 22 miles per hour toward our location with reported winds of 145 miles per hour. It had skidded right across the Everglades and was now charging north through the Gulf of Mexico. This didn't worry me because I knew I could ride it out in the port of New Orleans. Earlier I had boasted that I hoped the hurricane would hit New Orleans so I could see it firsthand. I felt safe on a tug because it was designed with watertight doors that could withstand heavy seas. Young and stupid, little did I know that I would almost lose my life when it hit.

It was Thursday afternoon as we moved further south in the canal to a set of locks that led to the Mississippi. The red lights on the locks were flashing, which meant that we couldn't enter the locks. It was not unusual due to traffic in the canal, which sometimes backed up the ships in lines that took four to five hours to get through. We tied up to a wharf and the winds began to pick up with the coming of nightfall. An hour later we heard something hit the side of the boat and saw that it was our AM radio aerial. Since we communicated with the locks on the radio and it had been knocked out, we didn't find out until later that the locks were flooded and would not reopen.

We received orders by company's FM radio to "find a hole and tie up." Basically this meant we were going to ride out the hurricane where we were. We went back down the canal about a half mile and tied up at the Florida Avenue Wharf. When we tied up to this concrete wharf, the water level had risen almost up to the level of the dock due to the storm surge. Our boat was floating close to the same level as the wharf. About 25 feet across the wharf were warehouses with large steel doors that were rolled down and closed.

It was dark now and we were tied up behind another small river tug. Two large ships were tied up across the turning basin from us. A turning basin is a wide area in the canal so that ships can turn around if needed.

The wind now began to blow in earnest.

The captain and I were up in the wheelhouse and the other deckhand was down below sleeping.

"Joe, watch those two ships on the other side of the basin," the captain said to me. "If they break loose we'll have to get off the boat because they could sink us."

He then went below to get a little rest. It was about 10 pm.

The wind was blowing very hard but I thought there would be little chance of those ships coming loose. Watching the storm from inside the wheelhouse two stories above street level was surreal. The wind was now blowing against our tug at more than 100 miles per hour, and the sound was a roar like I had never heard before. I was sitting in the captain's chair with a commanding view of the city of New Orleans. I watched as the lights in the city began to go out. The wind was blowing the high voltage power electric transmission lines together and when they touched there was a bright green flash. It could have been New Year's Eve fireworks except for the wind. Looking over to my right at the large warehouses lining the wharf I noticed that the large steel roll-down doors had been blown in and were flapping in the wind like a flag. There's no way to get through that door, I thought.

The tug was tied to the leeward side of the canal which meant that the wind was pushing us against the wharf. The ships across the canal would come our way if they broke loose.

At 11 pm the captain bounded into the wheelhouse and shouted to me to hurry and wake up Ben, the other deckhand, because we had to get off the boat immediately. I looked over at the two ships that had been tied up and to my amazement, they were now floating in the middle of the basin and headed our way fast. Two tremendous unlighted black ships were bearing down on us. The only light to see them by was furnished by the electric wires popping and flashing when they blew against each other. The wind was even stronger now at about 120 miles an hour. As I looked out at the wharf and warehouse, the only place we could go, the doors and windows were blown in and the whole building was shaking. I could no longer see the wharf because the water level had risen above it, but the tops of the four-foot bollards which we used to tie up the boats were just visible above the water.

All three of us pushed open the wheelhouse door against the screaming wind and made our way down the steps to the deck. We climbed over the side of our tug and down onto the wharf holding on to anything we could grab for every inch of the way. If we hadn't been bracing ourselves, we would have surely been carried away by the wind. Everything was blowing by — metal roofing, debris and raindrops that felt like bullets when they hit our faces. We faced the wind and bent over at the waist just to keep from being blown away. The water was waist-deep on the wharf. I didn't see how we could make it the 10 yards to the warehouse. When we had made it about halfway to the warehouse, we could see the large ships drifting in quickly in the raging storm. The surroundings were lit only by the eerie electric light of wires crashing and colliding. It was impossible to hear anything except wind. It was like Hell itself.

One of the ships hit the wharf directly ahead of our boat, and suddenly we could hear metal grinding above the wind as the ship's blade-like bow plowed into the concrete wharf and warehouses. The black hull loomed over us and I thought this was it. Trudging through the water with no place to go to get safe, the wind screamed through the rigging of the ship 100 feet above us. I stayed bent over to stay on my feet, with rain and all kinds of debris pelting my face. It seemed there was no way out of this.

We watched the ship as it came to a stop and smashed the warehouse. The stern of this ship began to swing away so we climbed back over the railing and into our boat for the time being. We really had no other place to go. Soaked through and through we went up into the wheelhouse where we were standing in ankle-deep water because the door had blown open. We watched the ships with our searchlight. We wondered whether we would have to get off again. It was almost midnight and the wind was blowing at its full force of nearly 145 miles per hour. The window panes were shaking badly and I thought they would surely break, but they didn't. The wind was so strong blowing through the superstructure of the ships towering over us that it screamed like a jet engine.

The other ship that had come loose had blown further up the canal. It was hard to see, but it seemed it was clear of our tug. I was scared now. There hadn't been time before in this ordeal, and I prayed. Our boat was leaning over the wharf from the force of the wind. We kept watching the ships, just standing there in our life jackets.

Then, in this raging storm, it suddenly became absolutely calm. No wind, a clear sky and twinkling stars! Dreamlike we gazed out the windows. This was the eye of the hurricane. This calm only lasted two or three minutes and then the backside of Betsy hit us with her full fury. The wind now blew in the opposite direction.

The captain said to us, "Now that the wind has changed direction, the stern of the ship ahead of us is going to swing around and crush us for sure."

Even though the ships ahead of us were only 100 yards away, it was impossible to see them and the other loose barges except when the wind and rain slacked up a little bit between gusts.

At about 1:30 am what we had been dreading

happened. The ship began to swing around toward us. It came fast so we had to get off quickly. Out the wheelhouse door and down the stairs into the howling storm we went again. On the deck, bending over, we climbed over the railing of our tug and onto the flooded wharf again. In the middle of the wharf, we watched the ship nearest to us swing around, feeling certain our tug would be crushed and sunk. I had only taken my wallet. It's funny what you grab for at a time like this. I believed that this was going to be my fate, to stand out on the middle of this wharf as long as I could and then be swept away.

A coal barge had blown up beside our boat in the meantime. Acting as a buffer, the barge now protected our tug as the enormous ship swung around and stopped as it pushed the barge. Our boat was now sandwiched between the wharf and the barge with the ship now stopped beside the barge. Our boat wasn't sunk so again we climbed back aboard in the furious storm.

I kept watch so the captain and Ben could go down to sleep. The wind raged on for another hour or so as the massive ship beside us was tilted over slightly toward us from the force of the wind. As I watched, the tug that was tied up directly ahead of us, turned on its searchlight. Through the furious pelting rain the beam of light pointed forward to a solid black in front of their boat. The bright shaft of light remained pointed forward a few seconds then slowly began to pan up the ship's side that was hanging completely over the boat. The ship's blade-like bow had hit the wharf just 18 inches in front of their boat. After another hour or so the wind began to abate, down to 40-50 mph, nothing like it was before. It was almost daylight — what a night! — we would be safe now.

Later that morning, after the storm had passed and water had receded off the wharf, I walked up to the tug directly in front of us and went on board. Two crewman were in the galley, and we got to talking. I listened to something quite surprising.

Jerry, one of their deckhands, said, "You know we were really shocked when we turned on the light and saw the ship hanging over us. We had all been asleep before getting up and turning on the light. That ship could have cut us in half!"

I guess we had a pretty smart captain on our boat. Getting off in the middle of a hurricane was no picnic, but what if we had been like that boat and slept? We might have been cut in half and sunk while we slept.

Finding My Partner

During spring break at vet school, I came home from Auburn. I visited my mother at St. Joseph's Hospital in Tampa, where she was recovering from cataract surgery. She was sharing a room with a very pretty girl named Dolores, or Dee, as she liked to be called. My mother introduced me to her. We talked over the next few days that I came to visit my mother. She had a serious leg infection, for which the doctors were even considering amputation to stop the infection.

Dee was 22 years old at the time, working as an administrative assistant at the American Cancer Society, and living with her parents and younger sibling in the Baycrest neighborhood of Tampa. Dee had been bitten by a mosquito on her knee, and then had aggravated the bite while playing hopscotch with her nine-year-old sister. After arriving home from work in her stylish pencil skirt and heels, little Karen had asked her big sister to join her in a quick game. High heels on the bumpy pavement resulted in a bad fall, right on the already infected bite.

It was good fortune that she shared the same room with my mother. My life would be a very different if this had not occurred. I got her phone number on one of the hospital visits. Both she and my mother were soon discharged and back in their own homes, but it took several days for me to call Dee.

I wanted to call the next day after her hospital release, but every time I picked up the phone and started dialing the number, I began to think, what if she says, "Who are you and what do you want?" I went through this routine for several days until one day I got too far in the dialing and the phone started to ring. Oddly enough, when she did answer, she did ask who it was, because she thought I had disappeared.

Over the next few days we called and talked many times, and then I finally asked her for a date. I wasn't sure where I would take her, so I just told her I would pick her up at seven. I hadn't dated a whole lot of girls and was a little unsure of what to do on our outing. I took her to a demolition derby and race in St. Petersburg. Since she hadn't known what to expect, she was dressed in a crisp white dress and heels, which was not the norm for the races. She was a good sport and walked through the sand to go to the track. We continued to date from then until now. After 49 years of marriage, we still try to go out on a date every Friday night, although we have found a trip to the movies suits us better than a trip to the races.

Just Married

Seven months before graduation, Dee and I were married. We were married on a very hot August day in Tampa. Our vows were exchanged in a little white clapboard wooden building that had been used as an Army barracks during World War II. This had been remade to become a small church with two swinging screen doors for the entrance. It had probably been a mess hall during the war years.

I waited nervously at the altar, sweating in my best suit and my freshly-buzzed flat-top haircut. The music changed, and Dee emerged at the back of the church on her father's arm. She wore a white gown that stylishly stopped above the knee, showing off her beautiful legs. A pillbox hat and small veil rested on top of her wavy black hair, and she was stunning.

The ceremony was a blur, but when it came time for Dee to put the ring on my finger I put out the wrong hand. She slid the ring on my right ring finger. After the wedding we realized it was on the wrong hand. Luckily it was a small slip, but the marriage seems to be legal as it has survived nearly 50 years.

Our wedding reception was held at her parents' home. Another surprise was waiting for me when we cut the wedding cake. Our guests gathered as we cut the cake together and each held a piece of cake in our hand. Everyone started clapping, and Dee got this wide mischievous grin as she held the cake menacingly.

The crowd began to chant, "Do it, Do it!"

She did it!

She smashed the cake into my mouth and face and twisted. The crowd clapped and cheered even harder. I had not attended many weddings, and I had no idea this was coming or was considered a tradition. I thought she didn't like me. I've been to many weddings since and seen how much fun that tradition is for everyone. I should have taken a course on weddings before I went to my own. Fortunately Dee explained the tradition to me later and let me know it was only a joke.

We said our goodbyes when the reception was over and headed out for our honeymoon in the Smoky Mountains, getting rice thrown on our heads as we ran for our car. We drove north on that blistering hot afternoon, with a small trailer in tow holding all of Dee's belongings for our new apartment. We were in love and happy as a plum as we looked out the front window of the 1963 Chevy. I married into the car, and we could see patches of paint missing on the hood where we had removed the taped wedding decorations. We had a permanent JUST MARRIED on the hood.

As we rolled up the interstate the thought of a car breakdown was the last thing on our minds. Only two hours into our journey the car broke down outside Ocala. Apparently the trailer we were pulling was too heavy for our car and the transmission gave out. We were 20 miles south of the nearest town.

I pulled off the interstate and said to Dee, "I'll have to hitchhike into to town to find a wrecker."

This was a time before cell phones and call boxes so my only choice to go for help was to catch a ride from a passing car. I hated to leave my new bride in the hot car but I didn't have a choice. I stood beside the road with my thumb out. A red Ford sedan pulled off ahead of me. A portly middle-aged man motioned for me to get in.

"Broken down?" he said.

"Yes," I replied. "We have just gotten married, and I'm a student at Auburn University." "Let me see your student ID, I'm a traveling salesman and I always check. Never know who is out here hitching," he said.

After showing him my identification, he told me he was sorry for our misfortune. He said he would often pick up college students as it helped pass the time driving. Before long we were at the first exit. I got out and thanked him and he wished us good luck.

He had let me off in front of a small green cement block gas station. Still dressed in a long sleeved white shirt from the wedding, I found a pay phone attached to the side of the little station. I began calling tow truck companies, but it being late Saturday afternoon and everyone wanting to head home for the weekend, no one wanted to come. I was starting to feel desperate.

Finally I got a man on the phone, telling him of my circumstances he agreed to come and I asked, "When do you think you can come?"

He replied, "I'll be there when I get there."

I could tell he didn't want to come out, and I thanked him. I didn't have any other options. I was worried about Dee in the car beside the interstate, and I had no way to contact her.

It was enough worrying about my new wife in the boiling hot car but little did I know that the stress level for me was about to be ratcheted up even more.

I was a heavy cigarette smoker and tried to quit many times over the years. When I met Dee she had a very good job with the American Cancer Society. As we dated she had sent me pictures of lungs of smokers. I had decided that I would quit smoking the day we were married.

We were married at 11 am, just four hours earlier. Knowing that this was coming I wanted to get every last one in before I quit, so I'll bet I smoked two packs of cigarettes before that wedding ceremony.

For the last 3 hours, I had been waiting inside a gas station about the size of a large bathroom. Three things loomed inside this small area:

1. Myself

2. The gas station attendant

3. A CIGARETTE MACHINE!

As I paced back and forth waiting for the wrecker, the cigarette machine stared at me, as if to say, "Ah, come on, you need one. With all this stress, if anyone deserved to take one now you do."

It was difficult, but I managed to not succumb to the temptation and I haven't smoked anything since. It's not that I didn't have the urge over the next few months and years. It did get easier for me as time went on and eventually I didn't have to fight the urge. When the desire to smoke crossed my mind I would think of how hard it was to quit and I knew I wouldn't want to do that again. I had started a new life.

About 5 pm a dull red-colored wrecker arrived at the gas station. If I had known it would take so long to get back to Dee, I would have never left her alone there. When I climbed in the truck, the driver in grease-smeared t-shirt introduced himself as Jerry. As we headed down the interstate to get the car Jerry asked what went wrong with the car. I replied "the motor is running fine but it won't move, like it's out of gear." He frowned and said "that doesn't sound good, it may be the transmission blown."

When we arrived at the car Dee was sitting inside. Jerry hooked up the wrecker, and I got to talk to her. She said, "I thought you weren't coming back."

When we got back to town we learned that indeed the transmission was gone. Unfortunately we had to spend our honeymoon money to get the transmission fixed.

Dee told me later that while she waited on the side of the interstate, a state trooper stopped by to help. When he first asked to help, she replied, "My husband has gone to get a tow truck."

He stopped again about an hour later. On the third stop, after almost 3 hours beside the road, he offered to take her to town.

She said, "I'll wait a little longer."

He could tell we had just gotten married because it was

plastered on the back window of our car, just in case he had missed the 10-inch high bare metal letters spelling JUST MARRIED on the hood.

On this third visit the trooper asked her, "Does your husband have all the money from the wedding?"

She replied that I did.

Then he said to her, "Lady, he's taken the money and he's not coming back."

No wonder she was worried by the time I came back.

The next day, with the car fixed, we headed up to Auburn Veterinary School for our newly modified honeymoon. Auburn is a small college town in central Alabama. It's built around the university which was founded as East Alabama Male College in 1856. Auburn is known as the "loveliest village on the plains," a phrase from a poem that so well suits this lovely little town. During the civil war its buildings were used as a hospital for the soldiers and university suspended classes. This land grant college went through several changes since its founding, but in 1960 it officially became Auburn University.

The two main streets, Magnolia Avenue and College Street, intersect at Toomer's Corner, the absolute place *to be* after a football game. The founding building, Samford Hall, and the surrounding buildings are traditional red brick with white molding and trim. The veterinary school is located on the southwestern edge of the campus.

In August, when we arrived, the campus was practically deserted. Almost all the students went home for the summer break, leaving only the few Auburn residents that were not students.

As we drove into Auburn I said to Dee, "I know you haven't seen the little apartment I rented for us, but I hope you will like it. It's small but I think it will be okay for the small amount of time we'll be here."

We pulled into Warrior Court, a small back street off the main drag in Auburn. The first thing we saw was a large white two-story antebellum house. With large white columns it looked like a *Gone With The Wind* plantation home.

Dee asked, "Is this ours?"

I replied, "No, it's back here."

As we drove down the driveway to the side of the big house we could see a little two-story building in the rear that looked like it may have been servants' quarters in another age.

"This is it, the one on the bottom," I said as she looked at my humble apartment selection.

There was one apartment on the bottom and two on the top, and needless to say they were tiny apartments. I opened the front door of our first abode and carried her over the threshold into the small living room. A bathroom was on the right, a kitchen (only big enough for two people to stand at one time) behind that, and the bedroom off to the left. The bedroom was so small that the bed occupied the entire room except for a small path at the foot of the bed. To get in and out of the bed we had to crawl over the foot of the bed.

To add to the shock of a new place in a new town, just a couple of weeks after arriving, a murder occurred in the little town of Auburn. Nothing like this had ever happened in this small college town. The suspect was a student named Eddie Siebold, who had killed two of his girlfriend's family members, in a crime of passion. For the next two weeks, as we lay in bed at night, we would listen to the radio for news about the search for the murder suspect. The details of the police search for the killer were broadcast almost continually. Most residents believed Eddie was still in Auburn and on the loose.

As we lay there listening to the radio, Dee asked me, "There's no one in any of the other apartments. Are we safe here?"

I told her we were, but I was not so sure I believed it.

Each night we listened to the radio in bed, and only a

screen separated us from the outside at the foot of the bed. The windows were open as it was August and we had no air conditioning.

The radio reports went like this *"Suspect Eddie Siebold has been sited on campus at the ROTC dill field..."* and *"Eddie Siebold was sighted at 5:30 pm. He was seen in the Cary Woods Subdivision..."* and so on as the nights went by.

Our tiny apartment was pitch dark and very quiet. Outside the open bedroom window, we heard every sound of the night. When a beetle would fly into the screen we would jump, certain the killer had come to kill us. Some honeymoon so far!

Two weeks after the crime they finally caught Eddie in Florida. He had actually left town the night of the murders, so we all had done a lot of worrying for nothing.

Despite the broken-down car, the cancelled trip to the Smokies, and the murderer on the loose, we had a lot of fun on our stay at home honeymoon. It was a new experience to grocery shop, cook, and go to the movies together. All the pressure of studying was temporarily off during this magical time. We had never lived together or spent so much time together, and it was fun getting to know each other and being in love.

Later in the fall, Dee took a job at the Agricultural

Science Department as a secretary. Coming from a good executive position at the American Cancer Society, this was a big step down, but since this was temporary she wanted to do it. When she came home at night she had some stories from her new work place.

The three professors in the office were leaning back in their chairs, hands behind their heads, 'chaw' of tobacco in their mouths as they discussed their hunting expeditions. One of them leaned back and said to Dee, "Go get us a cup of coffee, hon!"

She had a hard time with this, and I told her to quit, but she said she wanted to stick it out since we only had a short time before I graduated. In the eyes of the Ag Science professors, this young executive was there to waitress more than help administrate. Dee was a great sport about this situation, and later went on to be the business manager of our veterinary practice for 35 years.

My school work at that time consisted of clinics--large and small animal rotations in areas such as radiology, pathology, and surgery. The three barns at the large animal clinic were for horses, dairy cows and beef cattle, respectively. As students, some of our duties were to care for the animals. We walked down the wide aisle of the beef barn, with the animal pens on each side, as we performed our duties. Most of the beef animals were Charolaise bulls, 2,000-pound white bulls with a hump on their neck. Being one of the largest breeds of beef cattle, they were very expensive bulls. Our professor Dr. Walker was a national specialist in bull breeding problems.

Apparently, they did not like being confined. As students walked by, they would back into the rear of their pen, then run full speed, ramming their head into the gate at the end of the pen. The tremendous crash of the impact made a startling sound as we walked through the aisle between the pens. The gates were made of steel pipe the diameter of a basketball. That much weight hurtling toward you only a few feet away is enough to make you think twice. They never did break down a gate but it would sure scare the devil out of me when they hit that gate.

This large animal rotation was a part of my final semester of studies in vet school. After the last class, my classmates were gathered in the hallway saying our goodbyes. We talked about our upcoming internships, which would scatter us across the country. For the past four years we had attended every class together — pathology, anatomy, physiology, poultry science, radiology, surgery and more. We had slogged through countless hours of cramming for finals. We had let off steam at parties together. We had laughed at the stink of each other after finishing work in pig sties. We had shared each other's struggles and disappointments, and celebrated each other's accomplishments. We had become a family.

Before I knew it, I was walking home from classes for the last time. That afternoon, I walked along the railroad tracks that led to our little apartment. On this cold gray March afternoon, I thought this will be my last walk home in Auburn. I had lived in this town for the last four years, and it was like home. My classes were finished. We were leaving in the morning for me to begin my internship. Dee was at the stove cooking as I walked in, and I reached around her waist I kissed her on the neck.

She leaned back and said, "Are you sad to be leaving all your friends?"

"I'm delighted to have no more exams to study for, but sad to be leaving my old friends," I replied.

First Job

The next day, the car packed with all our meager possessions, we headed out of Auburn to begin a new life. Having satisfactorily completed all my classes made this overcast morning brighter. Having the weight of classes and studies off my shoulders felt great. Each course in veterinary school was only nine weeks long, as Auburn operated on a quarter system. This meant that your grade was determined by only two things, a midterm exam and a final exam. Some courses, for example, might cover 500 pages of a very technical surgery textbook in nine weeks! If you received an F in any course you were OUT of veterinary school. The pressure, albeit mostly self-imposed, was there all the time to make darn-sure you studied well enough for each exam so that failure would not occur. The thought of flunking out after investing all those years had been a heavy weight. As we drove away it was as if an elephant was lifted off my shoulders!

The sun was streaming through the windshield, warming us on that cool March day. My beautiful wife was beside me as I headed out to begin my new career. At the time, our old Chevrolet had a front seat with no dividers across the middle, so my honey was snuggled up beside me. Life didn't get any better than this!

As we drove through South Georgia, the road wound up and around the hills. It was as if we were on an old wagon road of the past that had been paved over with asphalt. The other side of the divided road was straighter and cut through the hills, not up and down over them, indicating it must have been built more recently. I had made this drive many times and the countryside with the large trees, covered with Kudzu vines, was beautiful. I was thinking, "I'm going to miss this lovely countryside." The Kudzu vine was imported from Japan years ago and has pretty well taken over all the trees in the South. The vine has large leaves and is impossible to get rid of.

The old joke is: How do you plant Kudzu?

Answer: Throw the Kudzu seeds over your shoulder and run like crazy!

Turning to me, Dee asked, "I wonder what it's going to be like in Plant City, Florida?"

I would be doing my internship with Dr. May at May Animal Hospital in a small community east of Tampa, mostly known for strawberry farms. He had told us he had a trailer behind his animal hospital where we could stay free of charge.

It sounded like a great offer for us because as an intern, for the next three months, my pay would be only $50 per week. We had our backseat and trunk packed with everything we owned. There was no extra space in that Chevy.

As the sun was setting, late in the afternoon, the highway was framed in orange. We were pulling into the little town of Plant City. We found May Animal Hospital without too much trouble, and turned into the small, crushed-shell parking lot. We got out of the Chevy and walked into the hospital. It was a gray concrete one-story building with the tiny reception room big enough for about three people. We were greeted by Marie, Dr. May's wife, at the desk.

She recognized me as I said, "This is my wife, Dee."

She replied, "Glad to meet you. Let me go get Dr. May," as she rose from her chair.

As we waited we looked around the room, where Dr. May's diploma hung on the wall. A thin coat of dust sat on the frame, and two dog charts were on the other wall. Strangely, they were the same exact charts.

When Dr. May came in we couldn't help but notice the differences between him and his wife. Marie was about the same height as Dr. May and very skinny. She wore metal-rimmed glasses and slightly yellowed scrubs. She had a weathered complexion, business-like personality, and a raspy smoker's cough. Dr. May, on the other hand, was jovial in a quiet way. His build was like most large animal veterinarians—a barrel chest, big arms, and huge hands. He wore a plaid shirt, blue trousers and a smile that put you at ease right away.

As we shook hands he said, "How are you doing, Joe? Hope you had a good trip down. Come on back and I'll show you your trailer out back."

Following him through the hospital I noticed the smell that was typical of all animal hospitals, a kind of mixed aroma of animals and alcohol. (Over the past 40 or so years of practice, many animal owners tell me that their dogs can sense that they are in a hospital, even though they have never been to my hospital before. I attribute this to the particular smell in all animal hospitals.) We serpentined our way through the hallways of the hospital and out the back door.

Standing in the backyard, Dr. May exclaimed, "Here it is."

We looked at the trailer and then looked at each other in surprise. We saw a small travel trailer in the middle of the backyard. It was shaped like a comma, laying on the ground praying, with wheels on it. It was about the size of a Volkswagen beetle!

Dr. May went on to say, "This is our family trailer that we've used on vacations. I think you two will be just fine in the trailer."

We looked inside. It was about the size of a bathroom and it was not possible to stand up straight inside without bumping your head! There was a small bed on one side and a camp stove and sink on the other. I don't remember a bathroom, so I don't know what we would have done for that. Sitting out in the direct Florida sun with no air conditioning it would have been unbearably hot. I thanked him and told him that I'd give him a call.

Driving away we talked about the 'comma trailer' and decided to look for a more conventional living arrangement, even though it meant more money from our meager income. Later that day I called Dr. May and thanked him for his offer, but said we had found an apartment with a little more room.

Our new abode in Plant City was about a half mile from the hospital. The dark blue concrete bungalow sat behind a larger house with the stairs going up the left side of an unused garage below. The inside was not huge, but it was a whole lot bigger than the "comma trailer." We were newly married and *in love* so the cozy ambiance suited us just fine!

I have a distinct memory of that first bungalow. There was no air conditioning and facing west, it really heated up in the afternoon sun. When we arrived home after work it felt like a sauna. Dee had found a job working in the office of a tile manufacturer. Some nights, when I couldn't sleep because it was so miserably hot, I'd take a bath in cold water to cool off.

Dee commented, "This place is hot, but we won't be here forever. We can make the best of it."

In spite of these things we loved our new little abode.

First Day

It was my first day as a veterinarian. I was excited. I wanted to do a good job. Arriving at 7:30 am, I walked into the small reception room past the matching dog breed posters. Going back into the clinical area, the hospital was divided into many small rooms, as most hospitals are.

To the left was a door to the exam room, which was a small room about 8 feet by 8 feet with a steel exam table attached to the wall. Behind the exam room was the lab, and to the right of that, the surgery room. Out the back door, past the kennel, was a yard to walk the dogs, with of course the *comma* trailer sitting in the middle.

In addition to Dr. May and his wife Marie, there was just one other employee at the hospital — Alan. As I walked into the lab area I was greeted by a short African American man with a bit of excess weight in his midsection.

"Hi, I'm Alan Spence. Nice to see you," he said as he held out his hand.

His smile was congenial and his voice soft and friendly. As I would find out later Alan loved to talk, which might be expected, as he was a part-time DJ at a small local radio station. Alan was a colorful character in his own right.

"I'll show you where we keep everything," he exclaimed.

As I walked around with Alan, getting to know where everything was, I could tell Alan was going to be easy to work with. He was wearing a blue checkered cowboy shirt, a wide belt with a silver buckle and cowboy boots with his pants tucked into the top of his boots.

Alan's friendly manner put me at ease. I guess you could say he was one of those people you just wanted to stay around and listen to. Having worked there a long time, he had plenty of stories about the hospital. He told me that the previous intern, Dr. Iverson, had just about caused Marie (Dr. May's wife) to have a heart attack.

Alan recounted the story of a morning when Dr. May was out of the hospital on a farm call there was a dog in for a spay operation, but we had run out of the anesthesia. Dr. Iverson said he could *make do* with something else saying we'll use a euthanasia injection instead. Dr. Iverson walked over to the pharmacy shelf and took down the vial of euthanasia solution. After some careful calculations he drew out a measured amount in his syringe. Dr. Iverson asked Alan to hold off the dog's vein and proceeded to inject the liquid into the vein. With Marie watching, the dog lost consciousness.

Her jaw dropped, became even paler than she ordinarily was, and looked as if she had been punched by a prize fighter. Dr. Iverson, noting her agitation, slowly explained that the euthanasia solution was the exact same drug as the anesthesia solution except it was in a much stronger concentration. To use it the way he had done, he had calculated the proper dose and drew out a smaller amount. The surgery went fine and the dog woke up with no complications.

Marie was distrustful of interns. She was also always on Alan, thinking he didn't work hard enough and talked too much. The truth of the matter, in my eyes, is that a lot of the people came just to see Alan. It was his friendly, talkative demeanor that they found appealing. Alan was the most unlikely person to be working at the May Animal Hospital (he had been there for many years before I came). It was 1968 in a small rural town in the south and Alan was black.

The kids loved to see Alan and made their parents bring them just to see him. He had a gift with words and he made them laugh. I remember a time he was holding a dog for me to examine and the lady who owned the dog had brought her two children with her--a boy and a girl about 4 and 6 years old.

Alan said to the boy, "How old are you?"

He replied shyly, barely lifting his head, "I'm four."

After a pause he asked the little girl, "How old are you?"

She replied timidly, "Six, almost seven."

Then he said to her, "You're not married yet are you?"

She was at a loss for words. As her face reddened, she stammered, "No, I'm only six!" Then he said, "Okay, I'm just checking."

That's the way the day went with Alan, and the clients loved him.

It was my first day, and I went to the small refrigerator for vaccine to give to the first dog of the day. I opened the door, I was confused by the large object, wrapped in plastic, which completely filled the countertop refrigerator. Looking closer, I could see a large eye peering through the plastic, and realized it was a horse's head.

Dr. May walked through and I asked, "Where did the head come from?"

He replied, "Last night I got an emergency call just after midnight to go to a thoroughbred horse farm."

Thoroughbreds are a very expensive breed of horses often seen at the racetrack.

When the handler called he said a three-year-old mare was acting very strange, and for the past two hours she had been highly agitated biting at her backside and actually biting out pieces of her skin and flesh. Dr. May said when he got out there several of the farm hands met him and said they had never seen anything like this before. As he examined her, he could tell this was something very strange. She was sweating profusely and her temperature was 107 degrees. On the rump she had bitten out small pieces of her own skin and her eyes had a wild distant look. These things just didn't add up. He said he told the owner that it would be best to put her to sleep and examine her brain for rabies. The owner agreed, and Dr. May euthanized her, then removed the head to take back to the laboratory to perform a rabies test on the brain.

The next day word came back from the lab that the horse did in fact have rabies. Seven of the farm hands who had handled the horse had to undergo rabies treatment (12 painful injections in the stomach). Dr. May didn't have to undergo the injections, as he didn't come in contact with the animal's saliva.

You never know what you're going to find in veterinary medicine. I'm amazed at all the new things and people I see in this profession, but that first day I knew I was going to like my chosen life's work.

Pierre

One of my first cases in my new job was a little white poodle who belonged to a doctor in town. His name was Pierre.

When I went to examine him his mother/owner told me, "Be careful he bites."

When I felt his abdomen he tried to bite me and I asked, "How long has he been irritable like this?"

She replied that he had been that way for about a year. This was very unusual behavior for this breed of dog. After running tests and x-rays, I found that Pierre had bladder stones. Looking at the x-ray, I could see at least seven stones in the urinary bladder.

"This will require surgery to remove the stones," I told her. She agreed and handed Pierre to me.

"I'll call later in the afternoon when I finish our little buddy."

This was my first bladder stone operation, and the dog belonged to a doctor, and I was a little nervous. I began by giving him the anesthetic in his vein. After prepping I made a 4-inch incision in the abdomen and then a 2-inch incision into the urinary bladder. After draining the urine, I could now see the offending stones. I removed the grape-sized stones one by one. Their surface was rough and covered with sharp points called spicules. To rub them on skin, they would feel like sandpaper. They looked like miniature medieval ball and chains that might hang off the end of a club. It sure looked like they would hurt grinding around inside the bladder.

I removed them all and flushed out his bladder, then sutured him up and sent him home in the afternoon. Several months later, after he had healed up, his owner brought him in again.

At that visit, his mother said, "He is a changed dog. He's so nice now."

Examining him, I gently squeezed his abdomen and he stood quietly and didn't try to bite. The rough stones had been causing him constant pain and when they were gone he had become a new dog.

Gee, Doc, You Could Have Been a Real Doctor

It's funny how people say whatever is on their mind. As a new, wet-behind-the-ears vet, some of the things that went on in the exam room sure could be funny.

Outside the exam room I read the chart on an English cocker spaniel named Sport with ear problems. Sucking in my stomach to gain a little extra confidence, I turned the exam room door handle and went in. I was met by the imposing figure of Colonel Yarborough, a rotund crusty old Army colonel with an unlit cigar in his mouth. He had Sport on the table as he gave me a look that questioned, *who the heck are you*.

"Hello, I'm Dr. Priest," I said as I extended my hand.

He shook my hand curtly and said, "Where's Dr. May?" staring at me with a wary eye. "He's on vacation," I replied.

I could detect a slight 'humph' under his breath to that. Then, clearing his throat, he leaned over the table.

His voice lowered a notch, and he said, "How long did you go to school?"

I replied eight years.

He paused, thought, and said, "Gee, doc, you could

have been a real doctor."

I looked at Sport's ears with my otoscope and noticed he had pus down in the external ear canal. This is usually the result of a bacterial infection in the ear canal. Cockers are more prone to this infection due to the breeding of large, fluffy ears which restrict the air circulation in the ear canal which sets up moist conditions which are ripe breeding grounds for infections.

I explained to the Colonel that we would need to take Sport to the back of the clinic to thoroughly clean the ear canal, and then he could go home and would need to have medicine put in his ears twice a day to treat the infection. I then gave the ear ointment to the Colonel and took Sport. When I returned, I showed the Colonel how to administer the ear ointment by placing the tip of tube in the entry to the ear canal, dropping the plastic tube quickly, and grabbing the ear canal and squeezing it so that medicine goes down into the canal.

Despite their smaller size, dogs actually have longer ear canals than humans. The ear canal drops down, then makes a sharp turn inside the head, making it difficult to get medicine down into the lower ear canal, where infections are. Also, dogs will immediately try to shake their heads, just as they do when they're wet. I often tell clients that if they don't drop the tube quickly after putting the medicine in and massage the ear canal, they might as well squirt the medicine off their front porch.

After working with Sport and showing the Colonel the ear canal massage technique, he thanked me and said, "You're going to do a good job, boy."

As he left the hospital, I am not sure whether he was convinced that I made the right decision about which branch of medicine (human or animal) to study. I was surprised by his comment in my career, but it would not be the last time that I would hear it. Later on at veterinary meetings, my classmates and I would discuss this reaction that they had heard, too, (*"you could have been a real doctor"*) and have a good laugh. In fact we would kid each other at our veterinary meetings that *we could have become a RD!*

Twins

My first solo call as an intern was to Mr. Rabin's farm to see his Hereford cow with dystocia. This is the technical term for trouble giving birth. Herefords are a quite gentle breed of beef cattle with a white face and red body. This breed was developed in Herefordshire, England, more than 300 years ago, and was brought to the United States by Kentucky statesman Henry Clay in 1817.

Mr. Rabin's farm sat back off of a dirt road. The cow having trouble had never had a calf before. She stood near the barn on a brick pavement tied to a ring on the barn wall. Had she not been penned in the barn, she would have been down in the most remote area of swamp that could be found. In my experiences, this is the area where most veterinarians have to go and deliver the calves. Animal mothers seek out absolute privacy when preparing to give birth for the safety of their young and usually pick between midnight and dawn.

Mr. Rabin said, "She's been pushing, trying to have this calf for six hours, Doc."

I put on my veterinary obstetrical sleeve (a long plastic glove that goes from the hand all the way up to the shoulder). I put mineral oil on my sleeve and pushed my arm into the cow up to my shoulder. As I felt the inside of her uterus, I could feel a calf turned in a position that prevented her from ever pushing the calf out on her on. Human babies are usually born head first, but calves are usually born head first or back legs first. This calf was presenting with the legs tucked up in a breech position. I had to attach ropes to the hind legs of the calf inside, and then the work began. The farm hands and I pulled on the ropes from the outside and after 10 to 15 minutes of struggle, the calf came out.

"It's a boy," I exclaimed as I wiped the mucous from his nose.

Just as a human baby floats in fluid for nine months, so do calves. When the baby first leaves the womb, it is very important that the airway clears so that it can breathe on its own. It has always amazed me how God created the life cycle whereby a baby grows and thrives inside with nothing but its mother's fluids, and then instantly switches to breathing air when born.

Wet and covered in slime, the calf was beautiful and breathing well. I felt real good about my first farm call, and everything was going super. Mr. Rabin was happy, too. I started to wash and clean up my gear when a thought began to trouble me.

Dr. Walker, our large animal professor, had told us

over and over in class, "Always go back in, after a delivery, and check for twins."

Well, I listened to that voice, put on my sleeve again, and told Mr. Rabin. "I'm just going to check and make sure she doesn't have another calf in there."

I went back in, and after a little searching around I felt another leg. It was twins!

By this time, the mother was exhausted, and it was best to help her with this delivery. I put the ropes on the second calf and we began to pull again. This calf was much harder get out than the first. We had to pull harder and longer than with the first delivery.

When the calf finally came and was on the ground, I said with relief, "He's got a sister."

She was just as beautiful as her brother and the brand new twins were nursing on momma when I drove away.

Thanks, Dr. Walker. I am glad I listened in class!

Graduation

When my internship was completed at the May Animal Hospital, Dee and I returned to Auburn so that I could participate in the graduation ceremony in June. Our graduation took place at the Auburn University football stadium. Now it's a massive cathedral for SEC football, but at the time is was still a horseshoe-shaped arena known as Cliff Hare Stadium. There were about 90 or so of my vet school classmates who had begun the long journey four years ago, and now we were all together for the last time.

Here we were, all dressed up in cap and gown, after four years of living, eating, studying and partying together, and feeling kind of odd in our fancy graduation duds.

Sitting in the stadium waiting for the ceremony to start, someone from behind said, "Hey, Priest, you're not graduating today. Dr. Horline came by and said that there's been a mistake. You still have one class left to take."

My buddy behind me was just kidding, but it lightened the mood at this formal and bittersweet event. I had been a student for so long, that it would take another year after school was over to stop feeling as if I should be studying every evening. I continued to have vivid dreams of walking into class and seeing my classmates stowing their books under their desks. I would ask them what they were doing, and a classmate would reply that he was getting ready for the test. I would immediately feel panic that I had not studied for the test. It was always a relief to wake up and realize it was just a dream!

After graduation, I took a job at a familiar hospital, Temple Terrace Animal Hospital. This is where I first was introduced to veterinary medicine as a high school student. Dr. Robinson took a chance on me back when I was just a teen looking for work, and again when I was a fresh vet grad looking to start my career.

Dee and I rented a small apartment in Temple Terrace, and I began my new career on June 14 of 1968. My first day was about getting adjusted to this animal hospital, and on the second day, Dr. Robinson left for a three-week vacation. This was the time before cell phones and email and the type of constant contact that we now have. I was the new guy, still "wet behind the ears," and it was daunting challenge. I had to go into the exam room day after day and pretend I knew everything, when really I was still learning the art of practice.

After the first week, Steve, a technician, came and told me there was a cat sneezing in the cat ward. I asked him to move the cat out to a cage in the dog ward and clean the cage thoroughly. This was a serious situation for cats as respiratory diseases move quickly. The situation required immediate attention. The next day, the two cats on each side of the cage where the first cat was removed, began to sneeze. We moved these cats, also, and cleaned the cages thoroughly again. This continued until the entire cat ward was sneezing and the cats were very ill with discharge on their noses and ulcers on their heads. Many of the cats stopped eating. Remember, Dr. Robinson was out of town and out of contact. I was the only one and had to deal with the problem. It was a nightmare.

The cats were being boarded while clients were away on vacation. Most of the clients were unavailable to be reached, and could not come back and pick up their animals. We began to give the cats antibiotics and fluids and feed them with stomach tubes every day. Most of the cats responded well, and after a week, most had been picked up or recovered, except for two beautiful Abyssinian cats. These two were the sickest and had to be fed every day as they would not eat. And if that wasn't enough, they had developed ulcers on their heads, too. We tried every day to reach the owner, Mr. Wood, with no luck. After a few days, I was tearing my hair out with all the responsibility of the clinic and these two cats who were not doing well at all and I thought they might die.

Freida, the clinic receptionist, came to the back and said

to me, "Mr. Wood is here."

Suddenly it felt as if a hammer were dropped on my head. What would he say? I sucked in my stomach, put my shoulders back, and walked up front.

I said hello and said, "We've been trying to call you for a week and we got no answer."

He said, "Well, I've been on vacation. I wasn't home."

I said, "Your cats have been very sick. We've been having to feed them with a stomach tube for a week. I'm not sure they're going to make it."

In my mind I was thinking that Mr. Wood would probably be livid. Maybe he would ask that I be fired and perhaps sue me and even the clinic.

His mild-mannered response was, "That's okay. I'll take them home and they'll probably start eating for me at home. Thanks for all you've done."

The cats went home and ate, just as he thought they might. They healed and recovered just fine, despite my frantic worrying.

During the same time of Dr. Robinson's vacation, Steve told me that a beagle who was only there for boarding was dead in his cage. We tried to contact the owner who would be on vacation for another two weeks, but got no response.

Unable to keep the body for that period of time, I felt it best that an autopsy was done to determine the cause of death. Luckily, Dr. Robinson's good friend, Dr. Ray, agreed to do the autopsy with me so that we would have at least two opinions. He was nice enough to come over that afternoon, and we did the autopsy, and found that a severe case of heartworms had caused his death. At this time, heartworms were still very common and very hard to detect, except through autopsy. Preventative treatment was not available yet as it is now.

When the owner returned from vacation, I was again panicked as to what his response would be. I told him that we had no choice but to perform an autopsy and had found that the beagle died of a heart attack caused by a massive heartworm infestation. He understood, and had a previous dog that had died of the same condition. Again, to my great relief and amazement, he thanked us for our care of the dog.

I was mighty glad when my mentor, Dr. Robinson, returned from his own vacation! The next five months were a piece of cake compared to the first three weeks of trial by fire.

Army

It was 1968, and the Vietnam War was full on. The action may have been halfway across the world, but it affected everyone at home in the United States. The news reports each week gave the number of U.S. soldiers killed. It was the first time the American public saw a war broadcast on television. Now that I was out of college, I was due to be called for the draft at any time. The waiting to be called up made it difficult to make plans for my life. It was my decision to join the army and serve my two years so that I could begin my career in earnest when I was done.

Many men knew that military service was inevitable. It was not a popular war, and some men even moved to Canada to avoid the draft. I decided that this would not be a choice for me, as that decision would be one that I would have to live with for the rest of my life. Other men, like me, knew that joining now would be to accept what had to be. For that reason, many decided to go ahead and join. Spots in the Navy and Air Force filled up quickly, while spots remained, and the draft continued, for the Army and Marines.

I went to the recruiting office in downtown Tampa, and joined the Army for a two-year hitch. Dee and I headed off to San Antonio, Texas, for me to report for duty. Dee was now pregnant and we had a dog named Boogaloo. Fort Sam

Houston was the Army's initial training post for all veterinarians, dentists, and physicians. Since most of the group here at Sam Houston were drafted, it was a very diverse group.

We were issued our uniform at a small World War II-era wooden building and told to report to the drill field in the morning. There must have been 800 physicians, dentists and veterinarians on the drill field the next morning. Up on a platform was a career Army sergeant (he looked exactly like a drill sergeant you see on TV, short, tough and hat cocked down) who taught us how to march. He barked out orders, "left right, left right..." and the group would trudge along, never in step. As the days wore on the sarge would get more and more frustrated with the group.

With veins about to pop out of his neck, he would shout, "You guys are never going to learn how to march!"

As we shuffled along, one of the drafted physicians mumbled, "If they don't like our marching why don't they kick us out!"

After a month of training at Fort Sam the veterinarians were ordered to report to Chicago for an Army veterinary training school for two months. We never really did learn to march well.

As there was no Army base in Chicago, we were given a stipend, called a TDY (temporary duty), to find our own living quarters. Most of our class of veterinarians stayed at a downtown hotel that had been converted into apartments. It was 10 stories high and had two elevators, and about 25 of us from the Army veterinary corps were residing there. The apartment building had just begun to allow army veterinarians to stay there again. They hadn't wanted veterinarians for the past few years as there had been some trouble with army veterinarians in the past. We were told that some of them had had too much to drink one night and had ridden motorcycles into the lobby, up the elevator and up and down the hallways. Fortunately no one in our group had brought a motorcycle with them!

Our time in Chicago was spent at a school for Army veterinarians to learn the procedures of our duty posts. In addition to the guard dogs and horses belonging to the military, there were also many pets who belonged to the personnel on the base. Veterinarians cared for these animals, but were also tasked with completing the food inspections and safety and sanitation procedures for food at our base where we were posted.

Our little apartment was about 30 minutes away from the training facilities at the Chicago stockyards. We carpooled together and drove along Lakeshore Drive beside Lake Michigan in the morning and afternoons. As we traversed along the lake each morning in February, it was covered in ice and snow as far as the eye could see. It looked like the whole lake was frozen solid. In the afternoon, returning home, the ice had melted somewhat and there were large waves crashing upon huge chunks of ice on the shore. For this Florida boy it looked like icebergs.

We enjoyed our stay in the Second City, and welcomed our son into the world there as well. Joseph Robert Priest Jr. was born at Presbyterian St. Luke's Hospital on April 3, 1969, almost to the day that I was due to report to my new post in the Washington, DC, area. Just three days after our son was born, I had to leave Dee and the baby in the hospital (she was still recovering from a caesarian) and drive to the Pentagon, where I was told to report. I flew back to Chicago five days later and the three of us flew back to Washington. We went directly from the hospital to the airport, and flew to our next home. Looking back, Dee sure was a trooper giving birth more than a 1,000 miles from her family, going through a major surgery, then moving with a tiny baby 10 days later.

My permanent assignment was now outside of Washington at the Quantico Marine base. Part of my duties there were to care for the 30 riding horses at the base. One day

I asked Don, the private who worked in the veterinary office, to bring a manure sample on Tuesday from each horse to our small veterinary clinic to check them for worms. It normally takes a teaspoon of manure to do the test. The clinic building was no bigger than a large bedroom and located in a residential housing area of the base. When I arrived at the clinic on Tuesday morning, I found 30 large buckets, each full of horse manure. I guess he had misunderstood. I did the worm tests on the samples (I had plenty!) and dumped the rest of the manure in the hedge out front. Boy, did that hedge get green over the summer.

During my time with the Marines, I found they have their own special language. Late one night the officer of the day, or OD in military language, called me at home.

The call went like this, "Doc, this is Major Reed Base OD. We have a deer in bad shape that has been hit on the road. We need you to come out and put him to sleep."

I began to get dressed to go to the base. A few minutes later a second call came from the major. He said, "You don't need to come, doc. We dispatched him."

I was a little confused, and I asked, "Dispatched?"

"Yeah," he replied. "With a 45," (referring to his 45-caliber pistol).

Robbery on the base

My base veterinary office was on the main road of the base. One afternoon we heard sirens outside and went out to see what was happening. Several gray cars were racing by with men in gray jumpsuits hanging out the windows. It was hard to miss the machine guns in their hands as they sped by. At a Marine base, I had expected to see drills, but this was very unusual.

We found out later in the day that an ex-Marine had robbed the bank on the base.

As the robber tried to make his getaway out the gate, the sentry shot at his car with his 45. The robber was not hit, and he sped away, right into the tiny civilian town of Quantico City, Virginia. This hamlet sits just outside the gate and is filled with people mostly connected to the military in some way. Here the robber managed to take a nurse hostage in his attempt to flee.

Now let's look at this scenario. Quantico is a very large base full of Marines. There are only two small access roads in and out. There are armed sentries posted at each entrance. In addition, Quantico is home to the school for the FBI academy. The people in the gray cars, gray suits holding machine guns were the FBI Academy students.

They cornered him in town and he gave up without hurting the nurse.

Talk about a dumb robber. I don't think you could pick a worse place to rob a bank!

Moonlighting

While serving in the Army in Virginia, I moonlighted for a veterinarian near Washington DC on Wednesdays and Saturdays. Dr. Schrenzel wanted me for surgery cases because he was losing his eyesight and it was hard for him to do the surgeries. We got along great. He was much older and crustier than I was.

Not long after we met he told me, "Hell, I graduated from veterinary school before you were born!"

Many years ago fluoroscopes were used like x-rays are used now. This is what had damaged Dr. Schrenzel's eyes to the point that he could not see well enough to do surgery. Fluoroscopes are basically an x-ray machine in which the machine sat behind the animal and beamed an x-ray through the animal. The doctor or technician stood on the other side and looked directly at a screen to see the image. There was virtually no eye protection back then.

One of the surgery cases that I recall was on a ten-year-old white poodle. Her name was Tippy, and she belonged to a U.S. congressman. Tippy had what looked like a red rash on her stomach. She was given routine medicine for a typical skin rash and told to return in ten days to re-check. Ten days later the rash had not gotten better. In fact, it was worse and covered the entire stomach area.

I took a biopsy of the skin to send to the lab for the pathologist to tell us what was causing the problem. When the pathologist's report came back it was cancer. This was such a large section of skin to remove—it covered the entire abdominal area—that I recommended to the congressman to take Tippy to a specialized surgeon at the nearest veterinary school. After I had left a message at the veterinary school for the surgeon, they called back and said the surgeon was sick, so it was best to do the surgery at our own hospital.

So here I was, left to do the surgery. I was only a year out of school, just a general practitioner, and this was a very extensive cancer. To top it off, the animal belonged to a congressman. Talk about nervous!

The congressman wanted me to do the surgery.

I began to remove the cancer by cutting out the cancerous tissue plus a half-inch of the adjacent skin around it. I tried my best to pull the edges back together and suture them but there were areas that I just could not get back together. We treated Tippy for several weeks but her condition continued to go downhill and she was suffering. We decided the best thing was to "put her to sleep."

She was a beautiful little dog, and it was hard for me to put her to sleep. The congressman, his wife and two daughters were with Tippy when I gave her the injection. All was quiet in the room when I depressed the plunger and her body went limp. We all felt it as if we were losing a good friend. It seems like a little chunk is taken out of my heart every time I have to do that.

Booga Lou and the Log

My Army tour of duty on the large Quantico Marine base provided me with a wonderful drive every day. The drive into the base from the main road was 4 miles of the most beautiful sights ever presented by God. Huge Chestnut trees, over 100 feet high, lined the two-lane road. I loved the drive in and out every day because of the scenery. In the fall the autumn leaves were like a stained glass window with the sun shining through them. In the spring the variety of the emerald green leaves was magnificent. Winter brought the bare limbs and the inner sense that spring would be along soon. Growing up in Florida, it was great to experience the seasons.

Our dog Booga Lou was a 12-pound black poodle. She had a lot of spirit and loved to fetch. I always said she was a hound dog in a poodle's body. We liked to go to a lake on the base on weekends and laze the afternoon away throwing the stick for her to fetch. She loved it. I could throw the stick out in the lake as far as I could.

She would leap into the water, swim out and bring it back, drop it at my feet, step back and bark, as if to say, "Throw it again!"

She never tired of this. She would go on all afternoon. One day I was tired of throwing her stick and I thought I'd end the day of stick chasing. I picked up a nearby log about two feet long and threw it as far as I could into the lake, which was only about ten feet. Not the least deterred, she took off and leapt into the water, swam out and got behind the log that was twice as big as she was, and pushed it into the shore as far as she could! That was grit!

Frank Trimball – a Black Cloud over his Head

During my time in the Army, I wasn't doing a whole lot of real veterinary practice, and some of the local vets had asked if I could come and help out a bit. In order to do this, I had to have a license to practice in the state of Virginia. The Board exam for a license was given a few times a year in Richmond. On the appointed day, I drove to Richmond from Washington. An old Antebellum hotel was used for this purpose, and with its high ceilings and ornately decorated ceiling, I could imagine the characters from *Gone with the Wind* twirling round at a ball. I was surprised to see my old classmate Frank Trimball also waiting to take the exam.

In veterinary school Frank was the rebel. He would come to class with the mandatory tie, but with no socks. During his colorful life, he had been kicked by a mule in the groin, and shot in the stomach by a hitchhiker he picked up. What I remember most was a class vote we had. Our final exam for a simple, one-hour course on dog breeds was scheduled on a Wednesday. All of the other finals wrapped up on Monday, and we were eager to have the semester finished. We all lived out of town and were anxious to head home for spring break. The class could vote to change the exam date to Monday, but only if the vote was unanimous. We voted. Guess who was the only one to vote *no* to keep everyone in town until Wednesday? Frank.

Now it was a year after vet school, and I was in the lobby of the old hotel, waiting my turn for the oral exam. The ballroom was completely bare except for a small table in the middle with five veterinary examiners sitting at the table. In front of the table was a folding chair that the hapless veterinary candidate sat in to be grilled by the examiners. The candidates waited outside the ballroom door for our turn. Looking in at the poor guy being grilled in the chair, we were not looking forward to our turn.

While waiting I noticed Frank on the other side of the lobby.

"Frank, what have you been up to since we graduated?" I asked.

He replied, "Joe, you won't believe it. After our graduation I came here to work for the State of Virginia's brucellosis (a disease of cattle that can also affect humans) testing program. I got robbed at gunpoint just outside Washington D.C. My boss sent me out to a farm to test a herd of cows and I got into an argument with the farmer. He didn't want his cows tested and he took a shot at me with his pistol. I got back at him though by hitting him upside the head with the bull lead."

A bull lead is a steel device shaped like scissors with large nubs on the end to clamp on a bull's nostrils. This heavy metal instrument, about four to five pounds, is used to lead a bull when needed. Imagining Frank hitting another veterinarian in the head with a bull lead made me imagine that I was seeing stars.

"That's not all, Joe," he said.

I scratched my head wondering what else could happen to Frank.

He went on, "At my mother's house, the pony I was training reared back and the rope I was holding had become wrapped around my little finger. Look at this."

He then held out his right hand and I could see that half of his little finger was missing. He continued, "My boss sent me down to southern Virginia to straighten out a veterinarian that wasn't filling out the state brucellosis forms the right way. I went down there and read him the riot act about how to fill out state forms. We got into a heated argument and I ended up cussing him out."

"But that's not the worst part, Joe."

I was thinking, how can his story get any worse?

He said, "See that veterinarian at the examiners' table? The second guy from the end? *That's him*, the one I cussed out!"

I was certain Frank would never pass the boards, but somehow he did. Fortunately I did, too, and was able to continue working in Virginia while serving the Army.

Back in Florida

When I was discharged from the Army Dee and I headed back to Florida. I had looked around Florida prior to my discharge and had found a job at Dr. Cunningham's hospital in Seminole. I was fortunate to have been offered a few different positions, but chose this one because it was a mixed practice serving large and small animals. When I spoke to Dr. Cunningham, by phone we agreed to meet January 12th at 8am and I would begin work.

Upon arriving at my new job, I didn't see Dr. Cunningham.

I approached the receptionist and asked "Is Dr. Cunningham here?"

She said no and I asked when he was expected back.

"We don't know when he comes in. He may not come in for several days," she replied.

I thought to myself that that was kind of funny. I now had a slight dilemma. No one had shown me anything about the hospital, where any drugs were kept, how the procedures here worked and so on. I decided to just get to work and try to use my judgement.

Three days later Dr. Cunningham came in, greeted me,

and said, "Glad to have you here, Joe," as if he were welcoming me on my first day.

That's the way he worked. Dr. Cunningham looked a bit like Ichabod Crane. He was very thin and had a sharp-pointed nose and an inquisitive expression on his face.

He asked, "Joe, how's Auburn these days?"

He had graduated from Auburn 23 years before me.

"Doing well, but I'm glad to be finished," I replied.

I didn't bother to ask why he wasn't in when I came to work. As I was to find out he was a bit eccentric with a capital E. His family was quite wealthy and he didn't have to work. He smoked cigarettes continuously and had a very particular way of inhaling on each drag. He held his cigarette is his right hand by the thumb and index finger. The palm of his hand faced outward and his other three fingers pointing up towards the ceiling like some sort of ritual. He slowly dragged in the smoke and then blew it back out more slowly.

After I had been working there for several weeks, I saw that he would come and work for some days and then be gone for days at a time with no apparent reason. I also saw that he and his partner of many years, Dr. Murphy, seemed to disagree on almost everything.

I would hear Dr. Murphy say to a pet owner, "Cunningham doesn't know what he's doing. This is the not the way to tape this ear."

Meanwhile Dr. Cunningham would say to another owner, "What has Dr. Murphy done? This is the wrong medicine to treat pyoderma."

They seemed to coexist this way so I just did my job and stayed out of the way. It seemed to me a difficult way to practice, but it was not my practice.

Making a Pact with Myself

During my job with Drs. Murphy and Cunningham, I was asked to take care of the greyhounds at the race track. Dr. Murphy was the track veterinarian and treated many greyhounds in the hospital. Dr. Murphy had large hands and a muscular build as a result of his large animal practice for so many years. During the greyhound racing season, November through February, he would leave the hospital at 4 pm to go out to the track and work there until they closed at 11:30 pm.

During the day the various greyhound kennel technicians brought sick dogs to us for Dr. Murphy to treat. Trucks that hauled the greyhounds to the animal hospital for treatment were the size of a pickup truck with enclosed kennels on the back.

One of my jobs, being the youngest veterinarian, was to *put to sleep* the greyhounds that didn't run fast enough to be used for racing on the track. By the time the owners decided that the dogs couldn't make it on the track, they were often just a year old. A year-old greyhound is a beautiful piece of God's work. They are a canine masterpiece, with skin like velvet, and every muscle in their body is formed perfect without a speck of fat. To me they are as stunning as

Michelangelo's *David*. They are generally friendly and wouldn't hurt a fly, licking you with that red tongue. Watching them wag their tails, it is hard not to love these animals.

I hated this part of my job. It didn't take me long after being told to put these beautiful animals to sleep for me to make a pact with myself.

"When I get out of here I'll never put an animal to sleep that is not hopelessly ill or suffering or both," I promised to myself.

I have stuck to my pact for all the years I've been in practice.

Hanging My Shingle

After less than a year with Drs. Murphy and Cunningham, I made the decision to go out on my own. Dee was pregnant with my daughter, our son was two and we had no money in the bank. I had come from a modest home, and although my older sister and mother helped me here and there with some tuition payments, I mostly supported myself and paid most of my expenses from time I left home to go to college. I had graduated in eight years with no debt, and spent two years serving in the Army and supporting my own family. It was 1971, I was now working full-time as a professional veterinarian and making $12,000 per year. At the time that salary was more money than I had ever seen in my life.

I had always been a hard worker and a saver, but typically a new veterinarian can expect to work several years at someone else's practice before having enough saved to open his or her own practice. I had always preferred to do things on my own rather than rely on others. In my work with Drs. Murphy and Cunningham, I had asked for a raise to $15,000 after nearly a year of work, and was turned down. In addition, I hated the previously stated aspect of the work I was required to do with the greyhounds, and I had recently had a disagreement with Dr. Murphy over an opportunity to make a little extra money vaccinating horses after work. He later reneged on the offer, and I felt cheated.

I determined that Dee and I needed $20,000 to start up a practice.

I went to the local bank to take out a loan. I sat down with a well-dressed gentleman and began, "I'm a veterinarian and I would like to borrow $20,000 to start my practice." In my mind I was thinking that I was a qualified doctor and this was a safe investment for any bank. I expected that I would be granted a loan and would gradually pay it back.

He was very polite and said, "Here, please fill out these forms and maybe we can help," as he pushed the papers across the desk to me.

As I drove away with the forms I thought, this is going very well.

A few days later I brought the forms back to him. He quietly reviewed the papers for several minutes.

He laid the papers down and looked up and said, "Based on this information we could loan you $500."

I sat still and confused. I was thinking about the commercials that I saw everyday on TV that showed finance companies loaning $600 just with a signature.

I asked, "Is there some mistake?"

He said, "No, you have no money in the bank, no net worth, and uncertain income." I thanked him and left. Now what would I do?

We ended up borrowing $1,500 from Dr. Schrenzel, who I worked for in Virginia while in the Army, and we made do. I built my own exam tables, bought drugs and equipment on credit, and moved into a rented office space. Somehow, it worked out OK. It is amazing what you can do if you have to.

Reflecting back, it was the disappointments and frustrations related to working with Drs. Murphy and Cunningham that led me to take a risk on opening my own practice so soon in my career. Sometimes it's the challenges and disappointments that bring about a better situation.

Sam

My first veterinary clinic was in a strip of offices located on a busy six-lane road. Much of my practice was treating horses. I was the only one in the clinic, as I was just starting and did not have a lot of business. To take care of the horses I had to fill up gallon jugs of mineral oil that I pumped out of a 55-gallon drum in the alley behind the clinic.

One day I was out back pumping the mineral oil. I kept the back door propped open so I could hear the phone if it rang. There was no one was in the alley and I was half daydreaming as I pumped. Out of the open door walked Sam, a white miniature poodle, hopping on three legs. He held up his front leg that was in a cast that I had put on his broken leg the day before. Sam belonged to my neighbor who was a banker.

I knew Sam fairly well from the neighborhood and as he walked out the back door, I called, "Sam, come here, good boy."

I was only six feet away, but just looked at me. I took a step toward him and he took another step away down the alley. "Sam," I called, "come here."

As I took two steps toward him, he took two more steps down the alley.

I began to walk faster after Sam and the faster I went the faster he went. We were soon in a dead run, with Sam staying about 15 feet ahead of me. At the end of the alley, the street turned left into a quiet residential neighborhood, or right into the busy six-lane highway. I was praying hard for Sam to turn left. HE TURNED RIGHT! I turned right! He ran across the highway, and I was right behind him in a full run. We dodged the cars that came at us. Somehow we both made it across unscathed. Across the road was a large shallow lake. Sam never slowed down as he ran out into the lake and began to swim. I went right behind him and waded out to my waist before picking up Sam. He was still swimming like a crazy man! I don't know how we made it across alive.

Both of us were now soaking wet, and I carried him under my arm back across the highway to my clinic. I put the lucky dog back in his cage, and noticed the reason he had gotten out was that the cage door was not fully latched. I would need to replace that wet cast, but it would have to wait a few moments.

I collapsed in my chair. My heart was beating a mile a minute and everything from my waist down was soaked-- shoes, wallet and trousers. Everything was dead quiet in the clinic.

There was no one to talk with except Sam, and he

wasn't talking. The previous five minutes had been unbelievable—like a dream. Neither one of us should have made it across that busy highway and still be alive. I was completely washed out. I just sat in that chair for a few minutes unable to do anything. All I could think of is how quiet and peaceful it was and just five minutes before it had been pure pandemonium.

    I got Sam cleaned up and replaced his cast. He was happy. We were both happy to be alive.

Colic

As I mentioned when I left Drs. Murphy and Cunningham to open my own hospital, a majority of my work was taking care of horses. My first six years of practice was mostly treating horses and other large animals. Although I encouraged my dog and cat business, care of horses is what put food on our table in the early years. Not many other veterinarians wanted all the night calls that large animal care involved. Colic in babies is something that keeps mothers up at night, but it's not something you think would be fatal. In horses it can be deadly.

Colic, or as it was called locally, sand colic, is a big problem for horses in Florida. During the dry parts of the year the pasture grass becomes very sparse. Grass that's left gets shorter and shorter from the horses grazing. Horses use their teeth and lips to pull up and tear off the short grass when eating. When the grass is very short they end up ingesting a lot of surrounding sand as they try to get the last of this short grass. This is particularly a problem after a rain when the ground is damp. It's interesting to note here how God builds the animals differently. Cows actually use their tongue to reach out wrap around the tuft of grass, tear the grass off and eat it because they only have front teeth on the bottom. Horses use their lips and teeth to graze. The sand that comes up with the short grass settles in their cecum, a big area of the large intestine where digestion takes place, and throughout their intestines. The sand irritates the intestines and causes the pain and colic, and sometimes causes blockages.

Bacteria are a large part of the digestion of grass, hay and grain for horses. After the bacteria work on the grass in the intestines, the by-product of this digestion is gas. When the sand blocks the irritated intestines this gas, which is constantly being formed, can't move down or be released. The intestines swell with gas which has no place to go. This becomes very painful as the swelling increases. If something is not done the poor horse will go into shock and die.

My practice was mostly "backyard horses," or just pet horses, and not thoroughbreds, the breed of horses you see at racetracks.

It always seemed I only got calls for horses with colic between midnight and 4 am. I think most everyone went to see their horses after they got off work, and it was midnight or later before they decided they had to call the vet. Often I'd get the call for a colicky horse about 1:30 am. Boy, was it hard to get up and head out after only two to three hours sleep, but this is what I signed up for when I became a vet.

On one such night, I got to the farm and found the horse standing very still with his head down in severe pain. When I listened to Sporty's abdomen with my stethoscope, I heard no sounds. Normally there are sounds of movement as food moves through the intestines. This process is called peristalsis, by which the intestines contract in segments to push the food through the intestinal tract. The medical term for the normal sound of this movement is borborygmus, a Latin derived word pronounced *bore bore rig mus*. (I always thought this word sounded particularly funny when I first studied it in veterinary school.)

I asked Mrs. Rose, "How long has Sporty been in pain like this?"

She replied, "He didn't want the saddle put on him when we came over to the pasture about 7 pm. He's steadily gotten worse over the past few hours and at 1:30 we decided to call you."

After I examined him I said, "Sporty is very ill with sand colic and I'm going to have to give him a pain injection. Then I'll administer mineral oil to try to get things moving in his bowels to relieve the gas that's causing him all this pain."

After giving him a Demerol narcotic injection in the large muscled area of his neck, I began to get out my equipment to pump down the mineral oil as the pain medicine did its work. One gallon of mineral oil is pumped into the stomach using a stainless steel pump about the size of a bicycle pump. A rubber tube the diameter of my thumb is connected to the pump, and the loose end is threaded into one nostril and down the throat until it reaches the stomach. The hose is about seven feet long to reach the horse's stomach.

This is not an easy procedure. When the tube is threaded into the nostril and reaches the throat area, it can continue downward in two directions, either into the trachea or the esophagus. Meanwhile the horse is in extreme pain and has heavy sedation from the painkiller. Thus the horse will not react with coughing or gagging, which it normally would, if the tube descends down the windpipe. The trachea has a natural reflex to close when anything solid touches it, even under anesthesia. However, when inserting a large tube, it is extremely tricky to feel when that trachea closes and diverts the downward path to the esophagus to the stomach.

Therefore, it takes practice, experience and a very careful touch to feed this tube correctly into the stomach. If the tube were to wind up fed down through the trachea, then mineral oil would be pumped directly into the lungs, which could result in nearly instant death. Outwardly I tried to appear calm and confident, but inwardly there was always a fear in the back of my mind recalling stories of veterinarians who had made this mistake and the horse immediately fell over dead.

"Mrs. Rose, will you hold Sporty's head level for me?" I asked.

She answered, "Yes, but is he going to stand still for this?"

"He will," I replied. "I've done this many times and it's always amazed me that a big 1,100 pound animal like this will stand and allow me to put this tube down his nose. I think that there is so much pain with this that he somehow knows that we are trying to help him."

I carefully threaded the tube down without too much difficulty and pumped a gallon of mineral oil into Sporty's stomach.

"You will have to walk him slowly around the pasture to see if he gets some relief. It takes about an hour or more," I instructed Mrs. Rose.

I then gathered my gear and packed up. Driving away I looked at my watch. It was 3 am. It was another hour before I would be home, washed up and back to bed. I wondered as I drove by all my neighbors' houses and imagined everyone sleeping, where did I go wrong. All these neighbors--bankers, accountants, engineers, and more--have never had these sleep-depriving emergency calls.

I had to get up by 7 am to go back to the clinic and see appointments for the small animal practice I was trying hard to develop. After several years of this routine I began to hate to hear the phone ring.

After six years of almost nightly emergency calls, I had finally grown the small animal care to a large enough portion of my business that I stopped serving as a large animal vet. Although dogs and cats sometimes had nighttime health scares, too, there were more small animal veterinarians who could share the emergency calls at night. Despite the toll it took on my sleep, I still very much enjoyed the trips out to farms to care for cattle and horses.

Answering Service

"**@&%%#!!!" A very angry Mrs. Reece was giving me an earful on the phone.

Years ago I had an answering service to take emergency calls at night. There were many different people who rotated nights taking the calls for my office and other professional offices. Some of these people were more savvy than others!

The night I received this call I was worn out from eight days of continuous night calls. The phone rang at 12:30 am. I answered and the young lady at the answering service said, "Mrs. Reese called and wants you to call her back. Her little Yorkshire terrier Coco' has that slight cough again."

I knew this was NOT an emergency so I asked the young lady to do something for me. I said, "Would you mind calling Mrs. Reese back and telling her that I'm not home and you could not reach me?"

She said she would and I thanked her.

The next day Linda our receptionist came to the back and said Mrs. Reese is on the phone for you. I picked up and after saying hello to a none-too-happy Mrs. Reese. She said, "I got a call back from your answering service last night and she told me that YOU told her to tell me that YOU WERE NOT AT HOME AND COULDN'T BE REACHED."

Oh boy! She did as I asked her to do, *word for word!*

Could Have Been Dead

My visit to the "chicken coop" was at 10 am on a Wednesday to vaccinate Mo, a chestnut gelding, which is a neutered male horse. I had treated Mo before without any problems. I was driving my 1963 Chevy and as usual, I was by myself. The "chicken coop" was a low-roofed chicken pen converted to horse stalls. It was to the right and slightly below a narrow road. The "coop" was about the length of a house and as wide as two cars. There was a dirt floor passage-way down the center with small stalls on each side. If I had stood up straight I would've banged my head. There was no electricity and it was fairly dark inside, even though it was morning. The horses were kept in about 30 pens inside approximately eight feet by eight feet each. The owners of the horses were almost all girls between 10 and 16 years old, consequently everyone was away at school.

I concluded, after several years of horse practice, that after age 16 the girls found boys and their parents were left with a horse. I based this conclusion on all the calls I'd get that went like this, "Doc, do you know anyone that wants to buy a good horse, saddle, and bridle?"

I usually didn't know of anyone. A few months later the call from the same parents went like this, "Doc do you know of anyone that would like a free horse, saddle, and bridle?"

Back to Mo--I opened the trunk of the car and got the vaccine ready. I put on my coveralls and boots. As I walked into the coop, I could see the other horses moving around in their stalls in the low light. Mo's stall was halfway down on the right. When I opened the wooden gate and went into Mo's stall, he recognized me with a low muffled nay. He was not agitated and seemed quite calm. As I said, I had treated Mo several times and hadn't had any problem. I rubbed his head between his ears and said, "good boy Mo."

He stood still as I swabbed the side of his neck with alcohol. I slapped the spot on his neck with the back of my hand to distract him from when the needle actually went in. He was standing still. I plunged the needle into his neck, a technique that I had done hundreds of times. At that moment he exploded and spun around knocking me down in the dirt. As he spun and kicked out with his rear legs, in this small eight feet by eight feet pen, his hooves hit the wall. Each time he circled around, his hooves were just inches above my head and body. I wasn't down more than a few seconds in all. I stood up as quickly as I could, opened the gate and went out-- untouched!

I was angry, how dare Mo act like that with me! I threw

my gear in the car and I took off down the small road. I drove a half of a block when the realization hit me. I stopped and pulled over. Sitting there in my car, washed out, I realized that I could have been killed or injured and no one would have found me for at least five hours, until the kids came after school.

I remember that profound feeling to this day, as if it had just happened. God protected me. I drove mighty slow back to the clinic.

See — That Proves It

Thursday afternoon I entered the exam room to see Mr. Gant and his eight-year-old beagle Jack. Mr. Gant looked like a cowboy that had been out on the grange for two weeks — pretty rough. Jack weighed about 22 pounds and had a typical beagle tricolor. As Mr. Gant held him on the table, he said, "I'd like to get him all the vaccinations and a heartworm test."

I said that would be fine, and then proceeded to examine him, give him his vaccines and draw blood for the heartworm test. A heartworm is a worm about six inches long that lives inside a dog's heart. The worms shed microfilaria, which become new heartworms after several stages, into the bloodstream. When a mosquito bites a dog with microfilaria in the blood, it sucks up the infected blood. The microfilaria develop inside the mosquito, and reach a stage where they can infect another dog. The mosquito then bites the next dog and injects this infective stage microfilaria. These grow inside the dog and develop into the adult six-inch worm inside their heart.

I prepared the blood for the heartworm test and looked at it under the microscope. I saw no microfilaria. I pushed open the swinging door to the exam room and told Mr. Gant that Jack was negative for heartworms.

"See…. That proves it, Doc," said Mr. Gant. "The dogs don't need those heartworm preventative pills. I put a drop of iodine in Jack's food every day and that test you did proves that a drop of iodine prevents heart worms."

What could I say? He was convinced that was proof.

There are two kinds of proof that things work: scientific and empirical. The scientific method includes testing on many animals and comparing the results between groups which have received a variable, in this case medicine, and those which have not. This type of test is usually conducted at multiple universities, and the universities reach the same conclusions. The results are carefully recorded and analyzed and published in a scientific journal.

Empirical proof is the notion that *I gave it to my dog and it worked.*

This empirical conclusion is the same as if I were to blindfold you and have you walk across a busy highway. If you made it to the other side alive, you could empirically conclude that there is no need to look for oncoming cars when crossing a busy street.

A Slip of the Shears

Tracy, our receptionist, found me in the hallway between clients.

She said, "There's a groomer out front with a little white poodle." She said that she had cut off the tip of the dog's tongue when she was grooming him. I quickly went in the exam room to see her. In her purple scrubs she was frantic. The little poodle was on the table with bleeding from the front of his mouth.

Looking inside his mouth, I could see the complete tip of the tongue was off and bleeding. She said while trimming the front of his mouth he stuck out his tongue just as she was closing the scissors. She had cut off an eighth of the tongue.

"I tried to stop the blood but got nowhere," she said.

"I'll try to sew up," I reassured her.

I took the dog back to surgery and gave him anesthesia. I prepared to sew up the tongue. I placed running sutures across the tip of the laceration. The bleeding eventually stopped.

The scissors groomers use are kept very sharp so they can cut fine hair. I can imagine how the accident could happen to anyone. I never heard what the owner thought, however.

Mrs. Reed – Her Money's Worth out of a Rabies Vaccination

Some people are better at getting their money's worth than others. Mrs. Reed was a master at this art with her dog Penny.

In the early 1970's I was in practice with my partner Dr. Taylor. He and I would joke with each other about how Mrs. Reed could get so much done for Penny for the price of just a rabies shot.

Normally when a dog is brought into the hospital each year the usual exam is called an annual, which includes a full physical exam, rabies vaccination, distemper combination vaccination, heartworm blood test, and fecal exam (worm test). Back then this annual cost $36.

When Mrs. Reed came in she would request "just a Rabies shot," which the county government required each dog to have yearly and cost just $6. Mrs. Reed was a small, thin, swarthy lady with a deep cigarette voice. Penny was a tan Dachshund, who weighed about 24 pounds, and had medium-length hair and friendly brown inquisitive eyes.

This was the setting. Dr. Taylor or I would go into the exam room to give Penny her rabies vaccine only. It went something like this.

"Hi, Mrs. Reed. I see Penny is getting her rabies vaccination today," I said as I looked at her chart.

She replied, "Yes, doctor, a rabies shot only."

I said hello to Penny with a rub on her head, and I gave her the vaccination. I set her down on the floor and thanked Mrs. Reed as I began to leave the room. At this point she said, "Oh, doc, could you look at Penny's ear just a second?"

So, thinking it would be a simple one-second check, I reached down and lifted Penny back up on the table. I checked the ear in question and said, "I don't see anything going on in her ear." I then deposited Penny back on the floor again. I would say thank you again and began to leave again.

In a sweet and lower voice she said, "Oh, doc, her toenails are so long it makes her walk funny and I can't do them at home. You do such a good job with her here that she doesn't mind it. Could you trim them just a little please?"

Penny went up to the exam table again and I trimmed her nails, while thinking this would surely be the last thing to do to earn the $6 Mrs. Reed was spending. I put her down thinking this had to be the end.

She said, "Oh I hate to bother you again, but she has a little sore on her neck. Would you mind just looking at it and see if it needs medicine?"

On and on and on. This would happen each time she came in and Dr. Taylor and I would have a lot of fun talking about how Mrs. Reed got her money's worth out of the $6 rabies shot. I still miss working with him.

Horse Impaled

It was a hot Sunday afternoon and I was mowing the grass at home when Dee came and told me I had a call. Little did I know how this balmy afternoon would turn out, Mrs. Noviski was on the line when I picked up.

"Dr. Priest, you have to come quick. Something bad has happened to Tony at the fence!" she said.

Tony was a five-year-old Appaloosa pony.

I loaded up my gear and headed out to the Noviski farm. I enjoyed driving out in the country, so this call was a pleasure.

I arrived at the farm and I saw about eight or nine people in the next pasture. They looked as if they were in a panic. Mrs. Noviski came over and excitedly told Tony had had a bad accident on the gate of the other pasture. I got my gear and we hurriedly walked over. I couldn't believe what I was seeing.

Tony was on top of the iron gate with an iron pipe sticking out of his abdomen about a foot.

"What happened?" I asked Mrs. Noviski.

She replied, "We didn't see it happen but found him like this. He apparently tried to jump the gate and missed."

The gate was made out of three horizontal iron rods with vertical iron rods welded to each end. The weld on the end where Tony was must have rusted out over the years. When Tony's weight came down on it, it gave way.

I examined Tony and I could tell that he was in a profound state of shock. He had a weak pulse, rapid breathing and was cold to the touch. Shock is an extremely serious condition in horses associated with trauma and pain. The horse's body begins shutting down. The arteries begin to close off and blood circulation is slowed down. The body is deprived of oxygen.

"Mrs. Noviski, I am afraid I'm going to have to put Tony to sleep," I said. "He's in an advanced state of shock and with that rusty rod penetrating his abdomen there is no chance he will come out of this because horses are very susceptible to peritonitis or infection within the abdomen. Even if he were to survive the shock he will die of internal infection."

She nodded her acceptance of this situation.

"Can you do it now? I don't want him to be in pain any longer," she said.

I returned to my vehicle to draw up the pentobarbital to put Tony to sleep.

As I inserted my needle into Tony's vein he didn't move, even though he was hanging on top of the gate. Everyone was crying as his body went limp.

"He won't have to suffer any more," I told the group.

Mrs. Noviski thanked me for coming as I loaded up to come back home.

As I drove home I was overcome with sadness. Poor Tony was alive and healthy one moment and in dire straits the next.

Wendell

Wendell and I met a few years after I had started my own practice. My clinic was a small rental space in a strip of offices. It was all I could afford having no savings and with Dee pregnant with our second child. I was a one-man show. Dee helped me here and there when she could, with our son toddling around behind her. I was still doing night calls as well, almost every night.

One afternoon a friendly-looking man in a button-down shirt came into the clinic.

"I'm Wendell Taylor," he said as his hand went out to me.

"Joe Priest," I said, as we shook.

"I've just started my practice about two miles south of here, and I wanted to say hello," he said.

Wendell was about my height, ten years older than me, and wore glasses as I did.

"I do farm calls like you and wanted to see if you wanted to split the farm calls so we could each get a little sleep," he proposed. He had had a busy farm practice in Iowa before he moved to Florida.

This was like an offer from God. My head was dancing

at the thought of this wonderful proposal! From the time I'd begun my new practice I don't think there was one night that I didn't have an emergency farm call. I was worn down to a nub with night after night calls and I was very happy that he came up with this idea.

As I have already mentioned treating horses' emergencies can be a real grind.

The usual routine meant going to bed at about 10:30 pm, and then the phone would ring for an emergency at about 1:30 am. I'd get dressed, load my gear in the car and drive out to the farm (usually at least a 30-minute drive). Once there the owner would explain that his horse had cut his chest on the barbed wire fence. After giving the horse anesthesia we had to wait 20 minutes for it to take effect. After shaving the animal's chest and prepping the area I had to get on my knees in front of him and sew up his cut. Usually the lacerations were quite large, maybe 12 to 14 inches long. While performing surgery in this position the horse would fidget about and sometimes rear up on his hind legs and attempt to drive my head into the ground with his front legs like a pile driver. You had to be fast to get out of the way or be driven into the ground.

After finishing up, giving him an antibiotic injection and loading up my car, I'd head for home, another 30 minute drive. It was often 3 am before I parked my car back in my driveway. When I'd finally get back in bed I would need to sleep because I had to be at my clinic at 7:30 am to perform surgery on a dog. Sometimes I would lie in bed telling myself to go to sleep, but the harder I tried the slower sleep came. By the time sleep usually came I had to get up again in an hour or two.

After many months of this routine I began to dread the ring of the phone at night. When it rang it was like someone using sandpaper on my nerve endings. Now you can probably see why Wendell's offer was so enticing.

I took him up on the offer and, oh, how wonderful it was to sleep when I was off duty!

This was not the only act of providence that came about concerning Wendell.

We continued sharing our night calls as both of our practices grew busier and we became close friends.

Many months later I was outgrowing my small little office space and began to look for larger quarters. Just down the street was an empty physician's office for sale. I went and looked at it with Dee and we mulled it over for several weeks. During that time I thought to myself *what if Wendell and I were to combine our practices and move into this building since we get along so well?*

I had never said anything to Wendell about this.

It wasn't many days later that Wendell called me.

"Joe," he said, "I have an idea. Let's combine our practices and move into this building I found on Park Boulevard. Let me tell you were it is …"

I stopped him there in mid-sentence.

"I'll bet I know where it is. Dr. Streets' old place, right? I had that same idea to combine our practices and move into his building."

We both had the same idea, like divine providence.

We bought Dr. Streets' building and combined our respective practices over several months' time. Wendell was great to work with. He seemed to always have a smile and I found it very nice to have a colleague to consult with on difficult cases. We shared a successful practice for about five years, before I left the area to return closer to my boyhood home in Tampa. Wendell and I remained friends and colleagues throughout the rest of our careers, and I lost him to cancer about 20 years ago. I miss him greatly.

Dead Inside

Sonny, the eight-year-old Dalmatian on the exam floor, was very sick. Mrs. Wall, Sonny's mother, was a small dark-haired lady with a friendly presence and a thick German accent. "Sonny has been sick for the past two days. He's thrown up twice and now he doesn't want to eat anything. When I take him out to go potty he strains but only dribbles a few drops of urine. He doesn't seem to get finished," she said.

I lifted Sonny up on the table and felt the stomach area with my right hand. The urinary bladder inside was enlarged and very hard.

"Just as I suspected," I said. "Mrs. Wall, it looks like Sonny has bladder stones and they are blocking his urethra, keeping him from being able to urinate. I'm going to try to pass a catheter to give him some relief," I said.

I got a catheter and began to insert it gently into the tip of his penis. There are three common types of stones that can accumulate in the canine body. Gall stones develop in the gall bladder, which sits in the liver. Kidney stones develop within the kidney and are usually very painful. However, kidney stones are less common in animals than bladder stones. Bladder stones occur within the urinary bladder and are difficult to pass on their own for male dogs because their urethra is much longer than females' and more narrow. To make matters more complicated, male canines have a small bone, called an *os penis*, inside their penis (sometimes up to three inches long) that is grooved to allow the urethra to sit partially inside.

Some other species of animals also have this bone in their penis, such as chimpanzees, bulls, rats, and raccoons. When a male dog develops bladder stones in the urinary bladder, some of them may pass down his urethra when he urinates. If the stones are larger than a popcorn kernel, they are blocked at the bony part of the penis because this is a non-elastic area which can't stretch to allow the stone to pass. The longer this goes on the more stones back up behind the blockage. Eventually he is unable to pass urine at all. When the dog is unable to get rid of urine it backs up into the blood and he becomes uremic. This type of blockage is called uremic poisoning and creates toxic levels of urine occur in the bloodstream and lead to death if not corrected.

The catheter went in smoothly for the first five inches, and then would not go any further.

"It looks like he's totally blocked, and surgery is required quickly to save his life," I told her.

She asked, "Will he die?"

I replied, "Yes, if something is not done right away to

relieve the pressure. I'll make an incision on the bottom of the penis, where the catheter would not go any further, and remove the little stones that are blocking him up. Then I'll need to open his abdomen to get the stones out of his urinary bladder. I'll take every precaution, but it's still going to be a risky operation."

Mrs. Wall nodded that she understood, and left to wait at home for my call when I was done. After running blood tests on Sonny, the level of urine in his blood (known as BUN--blood urea nitrogen) was four times greater than the normal level. There was no time to waste as I hooked him up to IV fluids, administered the anesthesia and prepped him for surgery. This was going to be a race against time to get the backed up urine out of his bladder and restore his bloodstream to normal before he died.

First I made a small skin incision just behind the *os penis* into his urethra and found eight brownish popcorn-sized stones blocking him up. After removing these he could now urinate. Step one was complete, but it would still be a challenge to get his blood free of toxins in time to save him.

With him on his back I shifted my surgical drape to the side of the penis and made an eight-inch incision into his abdomen. When I opened the incision with my hands and looked inside I saw something I will never forget. Sonny's intestines were normal, but his urinary bladder was as black as coal. Normally the bladder is a nice pink color like the rest of the intestines and about the size of a large peach in a dog the size of Sonny. Sonny's bladder was not only black and enlarged, but when I lifted it up with my hand it felt dead, like hamburger meat that had spoiled. It was the deadest looking tissue I have ever seen in a living animal.

    I thought to myself that he would never live through this operation. He had to have his bladder to live, and this bladder would never return to normal. Having come this far I decided to go ahead with the surgery. Making an incision into the bladder I found several stones the size of marbles and removed them, all the while thinking this was a futile effort. These stones were the same color as I had taken out of his blocked urethra. After checking to see that no small stones were left I rinsed out the inside with saline to remove the tiny stone particles that were left.

    Now it was time to suture up Sonny's dead, blackened bladder. This was like working with dead roadkill. There was no feeling of living tissue at all. Living tissue has a pink warm softness to it, whereas this tissue was stiff, black and reminded me of spoiled meat. I placed the sutures into the wall of the bladder, knowing it was hopeless.

After getting the outside skin sutured and putting Sonny back in his cage, I was amazed he was breathing.

I called Mrs. Wall, "Sonny's out of surgery and starting to wake up, but I don't think he will survive. His bladder looked like it was dead because the stones had done so much damage."

She replied, "I knew he was bad off. I'm glad you went ahead and tried."

We kept Sonny on antibiotics and fluids for the next five days in the clinic. He made slow and steady improvement over this time and after five days I called Mrs. Wall again.

"Sonny can go home today," I said. "I don't see how he could have survived this. It's like a miracle. In all my years of veterinary practice I have never seen anything like it. I would have bet a thousand to one that he would not be alive today."

In her heavy German accent she replied, "Thank you so much, doctor. I'll be right over to get him."

We went back to the kennel to tell Sonny his momma was coming to get him and make sure he was nice and clean to go home. As we led him out of the kennel room, his tail began wagging faster and faster as he heard his mother in the front to pick him up. What a reunion--I don't know who was happier Sonny or his mother!

Sonny lived happily for several more years with few problems.

A Sinking Feeling about a Tough Case

Mr. Kennan was in the exam room as I went in with Buffy. Buffy looked pretty normal for an eight-year-old female cocker spaniel. Buffy was tan and white and a little overweight.

"She's been vomiting two to three times a day for the past three weeks. Other than that she's been okay," Mr. Kennan said.

It seemed like a pretty routine case of gastroenteritis so I gave him antibiotics for her and sent them home. A week later he was back and she was worse. I recommended bloodwork and x-rays. He said they could not afford both so he said I just want to do the blood tests.

The next day the bloodwork results were in and I called Mr. Kennan to tell him the results were inconclusive. He asked if they could try antibiotics a while longer as money was an issue.

One week later our receptionist Tracy came back to my office and said Mr. Kennan was back and Buffy was even worse. When I went in the room Buffy was laying down on the table.

Mr. Kennan said, "She vomits all the time now and she has diarrhea pretty bad."

"I think we're going to have to x-ray her," I said. "I'll x-ray her now, and you can pay me later when you are able."

I put Buffy under my arm and took her back to the x-ray machine. I put on my lead apron and took an x-ray of her abdomen. She was so sick I did not need anyone to hold her still while we took the pictures. I took Buffy back to Mr. Kennan and then developed the x-ray. What a surprise I found when I held the wet film up to the light! Inside the abdomen was a grenade-shaped object the size of an acorn.

I returned to the exam room and held it up so Mr. Kennan could see.

"There is definitely something in her stomach," I exclaimed.

"What is it?" he asked.

"I don't know yet."

We looked at it awhile and something gave me an idea. I asked Mr. Kennan, "Do you do a lot of fishing?"

"Yes, I like to fish. Why?"

I told him that I thought that the object looked like a lead sinker, and he agreed, admitting that Buffy liked to play with his fishing gear. I explained that I would have to operate, but it looked like she was very sick with lead poisoning. I explained that this would be risky. I hooked her up to IV fluids and began surgery to remove the sinker from her stomach, hoping she would survive the surgery.

After getting the sinker out and sewing her up I laid her on a towel in a cage to rest and recover. She took a long time to wake up. I had to treat her to reverse the lead poisoning for several weeks, but she finally recovered with no brain damage or blindness. Mr. Kennan was awfully glad to see her after a week in the hospital. I didn't get paid much for all the x-rays, surgery or treatment, but it was worth it to see the reunion of Buffy and Mr. Kennan.

Lead poisoning is not common in dogs. I've seen it only twice in my 40 years of practice. I've seen dogs eat many things like coins, sewing needles, rubber balls, and even a Red Lobster pin from an employee's uniform, but this was the only instance of a dog eating a lead sinker.

A Horse in Trouble

Thirteen-year-old Debbie Edwards called at three in the afternoon.

"My stallion is acting very strange. His ears are laid back on his head and he's very stiff," she said.

"I can come out and look at him at five today," I told her.

As I drove the two miles to her parents' farm, I was trying to think of what might be bothering him. It sounded strange to me. I arrived at the farm and as I parked I could see the barn behind the house where several people were. I jumped out of my car and put on my coveralls and rubber boots. I grabbed my medical bag and headed to the group.

I walked up to the barn and could see Satchelass, a young Appaloosa stallion about 15 hands. A horse's height is measured in hands. One hand is equal to four inches, and the measurement is taken from the ground to the top of the shoulders. A hand measurement is the distance from the end of the thumb to the end of the little finger. It's an ancient way to measure the height of horses, but it is still used today.

Debbie was standing next to the stallion with her father, who was a big man at six foot five inches tall. The horse stood very rigid and was sweating profusely. His ears were laid back on his head, and his eyes were almost closed. His nostrils flared and his lips were drawn back.

As I examined him he tensed up each time I touched him. I tried to go slow and gentle so he wouldn't get too excited. He gave the appearance of a sawhorse, with legs slightly spread. His jaws were clinched tight shut.

My mind was racing to try and figure out what was happening right in front of me. I remembered, from endless repetitions in veterinary school, that lockjaw was the hallmark symptom of tetanus. I also remembered that horses are more susceptible to tetanus than other farm animals. I wondered if this could be tetanus. I had only studied this disease in school, but had never seen a real case.

In our studies at school we had learned that tetanus spores are everywhere in a farm yard. It usually takes a puncture wound of some sort for the spore (the bacteria clostridium tetani) to be introduced into the body. This can be caused by a nail, a piece of wire on a fence, etc. Once in the body the bacteria grows and produces a strong neurotoxin causing involuntary muscle contractions. The toxin is so strong that an amount the size of a pinhead can cause death.

I turned back to Debbie and her father and I said, "I think this is tetanus. Unfortunately, only fifty percent of horses live through this."

As I was talking someone dropped a garbage can lid which made a loud noise. The stallion tensed up even more and began shaking violently. He reared up on his hind legs and fell over backwards. It was a bit like watching a small car turned up vertically and falling back on its top. When he hit the ground I thought he would be dead or at least knocked unconscious. He didn't die after he hit but laid on his side with his feet out and rigid. This happened so fast that there was no way to stop it.

After a few minutes we got him up and standing again. Generally horses are standing, even when sleeping. It is preferable to treat a horse standing to avoid being kicked. They do sometimes lie down, but standing is the natural state of a horse. There is even a special check ligament in their legs that allows them to stand and sleep with no effort. I gave him an injection of antibiotics and explained that I needed to go back to the office to collect the right medicine to treat him.

When I got back to my office and looked in the refrigerator I had only one vial of antitoxin and I needed 15. In fact, I would need 15 vials each day for one week. After many phone calls to my veterinary colleagues around town I found the 15 vials I needed and drove to the three or four clinics to pick them up.

It was 6:30 pm before I got back to Edwards' farm.

Satchelass's condition had not changed. I selected a 20cc syringe from my bag and drew up the contents of the 15 vials of antitoxin into the syringe.

He was tied up in his stall, and still sweating and rigid. I softly opened the stall gate and began to stroke him on his neck. I tried not to upset him. I smoothed his lower neck with my right hand and held off the jugular vein until it stood out. In horses the jugular vein is the size of a garden hose. I gently slipped the needle into the vein. He remained calm as I slowly administered the antitoxin.

I washed up at the faucet and told Debbie and her father that was all that I could do for now. I advised to try and keep things quiet and dark for the horse tonight, and I would be back the next day to give him the next dose.

"I'm having a hard time rounding up enough antitoxin to treat him," I said. "The normal dose for dogs is one vial and I need 15 every day for your horse. I am buying out every veterinarian's supply in town that I can."

By the third day of treatment he seemed to have gotten a little better. At the end of the week of treatment the shaking and clenching of the jaws had subsided to the point that he actually began to eat a little food on his own.

We all were talking and could not believe that he lived through this.

I was actually able to contact Debbie, after almost 50 years. She told me that her father had passed away and that she had gone to vet school and opened her own practice treating cats only. She had even recently retired. Wow!

I asked her where the name Satchelass came from. She said that he had a white patch the size of a satchel on his rump. It was an appropriate name. She told me that I was her inspiration to become a vet. She had helped me treat a neighbor's horse that was cut on a fence. She held the mare's head while I sewed her up. What a nice thing to think I actually inspired her.

Kittens on the doorstep

Veterinary hospitals are places where unwanted animals are commonly left on the doorstep. Our clinic was no exception. Our building was a brown wooden building with a large oak tree in front just to the left of the front door. As I came into work, I turned the key in the front door at 7:30 am and heard the tiniest meow from the bushes beside the tree. When I looked over there was a cardboard box by the tree. I picked up the box and inside were five grey kittens no more than five days old.

I took them inside to get a better look, and found they were in rough shape. What I found was that these helpless creatures had been brutalized by someone. It was hard to conceive why anyone would want to hurt these innocent little lives. The most disgusting thing was that their eyes had been poked out, some of them in both eyes and some just one. Everyone at the clinic went to work cleaning and treating the little bundles of joy.

In a few days, miraculously, they were doing better so we put out the word among our clients that they needed a home. We told them that it would be a labor of love because some were fully blind and some were half blind.

Now this is the part that I still can't get over. After the

word was out we adopted out ALL of them in a matter of four days. I'll bet we had fifty calls. It was a nice problem to have more requests than kittens, but that's not all. The most amazing thing is most of the people who called wanted one of the totally blind kittens.

I think I learned a lot about human nature by this event in my life. It seems like most people wanted to help the underdog first. It was heartening to me there seems to be there are more good people than bad.

Gnarled Hands

The greatest thing about being a veterinarian is getting to do something good for someone who really needs it. Mrs. Mallory smiled gently as I walked in the exam room. She got up with some difficulty and put her poodle Max on the table.

"Max is here for his annual vaccinations," she said.

Mrs. Mallory, dressed in a flowered green dress, was in her late sixties and had a warm friendly smile. The most noticeable thing I observed about her was her hands. They were gnarled and twisted from arthritis. In the years I had known Mrs. Mallory I had never known her to complain.

"You know, Doctor, he turned twelve six days ago and he's the best dog I could ever want to have," she said.

Max was small, black, with graying hair around his face and ears. Upon examining him I found cataracts forming in his eyes and several loose teeth.

"Mrs. Mallory, Max needs to have his loose teeth removed and his teeth cleaned. Those loose teeth probally hurt him when he chews," I explained to her.

She asked how much it would be for the teeth. I told her it would be an additional $65. She was silent for a few seconds and replied with much sadness in her voice, "I'd like to have it done but I live on social security and I just can't do it."

She was so genuine that it broke my heart.

As I finished my exam and gave Max his vaccinations my mind was buzzing. As I was walking out the door of the exam room I looked back over my shoulder and asked her, "Did Max eat this morning?"

To clean and extract a dog's teeth, anesthesia has to be given and the animal must be without food for twelve hours.

Mrs. Mallory replied, "No, he hasn't eaten today."

"Can you leave him for a few hours and we will get his teeth fixed up?"

She looked perplexed as she said, "…but I can't afford it."

I responded, "There will be no charge."

She was happy.

We kept Max and pulled several of the rotten teeth and cleaned the others. He did fine. I was as happy as I've ever been!

When she picked her boy up she thanked me and kissed him. Being able to do that has given me one of my warmest feelings of all the years I've taken care of animals.

Why Dogs Roll in Smelly Things

We had a dog named Chloe, a little white fluffball weighing only eight pounds. When she had a bath, she was bright white and as fuzzy as a cotton ball. I noticed that just after her bath, I could take her for a walk and she would immediately run to something that had died in the grass. She would plop right down and roll her back all through the decomposing mess. By the time we would return home from a walk on bath day, she would be so stinky that she would need another bath.

This instinct must be a part of a dog's genes from long ago. I have been asked about this strange behavior from baffled owners countless times, and have witnessed it with my own pets. In the wild, animals are always sniffing the air for the scent of a predator. A herd of wildebeests, for instance, will routinely crane their heads upward to sniff out any lurking danger, and then may startle and run off quickly to try and avoid whatever animal may be hunting.

When dogs hunt they roll in the most foul-smelling thing they can find to mask their scent and not scare off any prey. I guess our pet dogs still have the DNA to be prepared for the hunt!

Heidi and the Grass Blade

Some things are much harder to diagnose than others. My high school classmate, David, brought in his dachshund Heidi with a discharge from her nose. Heidi was a wee bit overweight with a beautiful brown haircoat. He said she had been sneezing for about a week. When I examined her she had a clear discharge from her right nostril. Everything else on the physical exam was normal. I looked up inside the nostrils as far as I could, which is only about one-fourth of an inch, but didn't see anything.

The sinuses, which are located just behind the nose, probably comprise one third of the head. In dachshunds, with their long noses, the sinuses comprise even more than that. The sinuses are folds of moist skin that filter dust and other objects out of the air before it reaches the lungs and add moisture to the air. As you look up the nose into the sinuses there is not much to be seen. They look like the pages of a phone book on its side. I couldn't see anything other than a slight redness inside the nostril.

My diagnosis was rhinitis or inflammation in the sinus of Heidi's nose. I gave David medicine for rhinitis to give her. Two weeks later when I examined her there was no response to the medicine.

I sent Heidi to a specialist and he x-rayed her head, and did every test and treatment that was appropriate--all to no avail. After months of testing and treatment David decided to just live with Heidi's runny nose. I really didn't see Heidi over the next six months except for a routine vaccine. She had that runny nose every time I saw her, and David and I had just accepted that she was going to have a runny nose for the unforeseen future.

More than half a year after this had begun, David arrived back at the clinic with Heidi. Something green sticking out of her right nostril. When I pulled on the object I pulled out a two inch blade of grass. It came out in one long piece, intact, and still green. After that simple removal, Heidi's nose problem went away and never came back. The body's reaction to an insult (or foreign object) is to produce mucus and with the aid of tiny cilia (like tiny fingers) to push the debris outward through the nostrils. The body was trying but the grass blade was too large to move quickly in this process. Normally sneezing would remove an object, but in this case it hadn't worked.

This is one of the strangest things I've ever seen. I would have never believed this except that I know that it happened. Sniffing around in the grass, as dogs do, she must have pushed her head down, at just the perfect angle, on a blade of grass. The grass blade was then lodged far enough up the nose so that it could not be seen. A grass blade does not show up in x-rays and that's why the specialist couldn't find it. How it was still green after all that time I will never understand!

Bubbie and Fenny

Fenny was a well-behaved, beautiful Great Dane with a majestic presence. He weighed about 145 pounds. He was as gentle as a lamb, and his auburn haircoat had a sheen that glistened as if sun light was coming from within. Every time he came in the clinic it was a joy for all of us to see him, and it was his disposition that we liked the most. He truly wouldn't hurt a fly--except in a certain circumstance which I'll describe below.

Mrs. Royal, a friendly petite lady, was mother to two dogs—Fenny and Bubbie. She was married to an airline pilot and her hobby was the dogs and dog shows. She made the best life for those dogs they could ever imagine. She had blonde hair and about the friendliest smile you would every see. She probably weighed about half of what Fenny weighed.

Bubbie was an off-white poodle mix who weighed about 12 pounds. He always held his head to the right side with his lower jaw stuck out, exposing his bottom teeth. He was blind in the right eye and walked a little sideways. His hair was course and unruly, not the usual curls you see in the fancy poodles. Bubbie had had an overdose of a strong flea medication at another hospital three years before and, according to Mrs. Royal, it had left him in this condition.

Mrs. Royal rushed in the clinic on a Friday morning with Bubbie, who had a large laceration of his skin about five inches long on his right side.

I asked her what happened, and she said it was Fenny.

I was puzzled and inquired, "Fenny? He doesn't seem the type to do this?"

"Oh no, he's not the type. It's Bubbie, he won't leave Fenny alone, he goes after him all the time and Fenny had just had enough, and he bit back."

I took Bubbie in and sutured him up and all was well.

Eight months later, Tracy, our receptionist, came to the back and said, "Mrs. Royal is up front with Bubbie."

Out I went to see what was going on now. I examined Bubbie and found that he had a large laceration on his neck. I looked at Mrs. Royal. She looked at me. I could tell without asking her that sure enough, it was Fenny who had done it again.

Mrs. Royal said, "You would think he would learn his lesson. But no, he just won't leave Fenny alone!"

We got him sutured back together again. Guess he didn't know or care that Fenny outweighed him by a mere one hundred and thirty-three pounds.

Bubbie's a fighter--sort of a dog version of Rocky. I

wonder a lot what the dogs are thinking. I'd love to find out.

In the natural world of dogs, when the larger, older or male dog confronts another dog, the other dog would either fight or submit. Typically the dominate dog might put his paw on top of the smaller dog's head. The smaller dog would submit by rolling on its back and urinating. This indicates to the dominate dog that the smaller dog will not fight back and this behavior would save the life of the smaller dog by preventing a fight that the smaller dog would likely lose.

When humans began domesticating dogs, they became the dominate animal, as they are larger and tower over a dog. Also, humans typically greet a dog by petting the top of a dog's head, and to some dogs this is a question of dominance in which dogs choose to fight back and bite, or squat and submit by urinating as a submission sign. Throwing humans into the canine mix sometimes confuses the natural order of dominance and submission among dogs.

In Bubbie and Fenny's case, Bubbie was the older dog, although much smaller. Perhaps in the dog order, Bubbie would attempt to become the dominate dog. As with humans, some animals are just born differently.

Olive

When I entered the exam room Mrs. Cramer had Olive on the table.

"Dr. Priest, Olive has been feeling bad for the past two weeks and seems to be getting worse. I try to feed her but she won't eat very well and is now vomiting," explained Mrs. Cramer.

Olive looked up at me with dark eyes that said she was not feeling good. She was a black, 11-year-old poodle, with a dull haircoat that was tangled and dry. She weighed about 10 pounds.

Mrs. Cramer went on to say, "She has a discharge leaking from her vagina that looks like pus."

Mrs. Cramer was a petite lady with an infectious personality, and she had about eight or nine dogs. She had had a stroke several years ago and it had left her with problems using her hands. She loved animals. Any stray that needed a home would find it with her even though she didn't have much money. I liked her spunk. She didn't let those problems get her down.

I asked, "Has Olive been spayed?"

"No, she hasn't. I've wanted to get that done but I haven't had the money," she replied.

After blood tests and physical I was able to find out what was causing Olive to be so sick. I had Mrs. Cramer return to the exam room.

"Olive has pyometra and needs to be operated on right away."

She asked, "What's that?"

I explained, "She has developed pus in her uterus. A healthy dog's womb is shaped like a Y and has two horns, each one about the size of a pencil and four inches long. When engorged with pus, as with pyometra, the horns swell to the size of a fat sausage."

"How did she get this?" she asked.

I explained, "A dog's heat cycle, or menstrual cycle, occurs every six months. The inside wall of the uterus prepares for impregnation from the sperm from the male dog. If there is no sperm the lining of the wall of the uterus dissolves and the uterus prepares for the next cycle as the blood and debris from the uterus wall is expelled out of the body through the vagina. As Olive has gotten older, 12 years being the average lifespan of all dogs, the muscles in her body have less tone and begin to sag."

The uterus, normally very muscular and prepared to

accommodate four to six puppies, begins to sag also. Looking at Olive from the side the uterus inside would be like a hammock. When this happens some of the blood can't get out and is left trapped in the bottom of the hammock of the uterus. Because the blood is still in her uterus after the time it should have been expelled, her body recognizes that trapped blood as something that is not supposed to be there and sends in white blood cells to clean it up. The white blood cells surround each blood cell and phagocytize (eat) it and what remains of the blood cells and white blood cells is pus. The way these things work is a miracle, it still amazes me that God could build all this information in only ONE tiny cell at the beginning of every living thing.

The pus that collects is a sterile pus because the white blood cells were not attacking bacteria from outside the body as they normally do, but Olive's own tissue and blood. Therefore this pus collects so silently and insidiously, that by the time symptoms occur there may be as much as seven pounds of pus in the uterus.

"When will you operate?" she asked.

"I will have to do it today. If I wait she may die," I replied.

I began Olive's operation at 2:30 that afternoon and when I opened her up there was almost two pounds of pus in her uterus. I removed the swollen uterus inside of her. It required delicate surgery because handling the uterus too roughly would cause the fragile tissue to break and pus to be released into the abdomen. Usually death follows quickly if this happens.

She was very slow to come out of the anesthesia. Her condition was so bad I didn't think she would live more than an hour after the surgery.

I called Mrs. Cramer and said, "The surgery is finished but she is not off the critical list yet. I'll take her home with me tonight to keep watch on her." I often took very sick animals home with me because having a small clinic I had no one staying there overnight.

When I left that evening I bundled Olive up in a blanket, and she was barely conscious. On the way home, curled up on my lap, she looked up at me with dark sunken eyes, even though she couldn't lift her head, as if to say please help me.

At home I put her down on the blanket in our laundry room with a bowl of water. Our dog, Sweet Pea, was curious to see who our new visitor was. Sweet Pea, a white bichon frise, the same size as Olive, walked into the laundry room and sniffed around Olive, who could just barely lift her head.

I told my wife Dee, "Sweet Pea is Olive's nurse

tonight." Sweet Pea went in and out several times to check on her patient. After several hours when I felt Olive was awake enough, I gave her a few pieces of chicken but she didn't have much interest. A little later I went back to check on her and her nurse Sweet Pea was not only checking on her but she was sampling her food. Her nurse had eaten her patient's chicken.

At midnight I looked in on her and she looked up with sad eyes, which I could tell indicated that she felt bad. I knew the longer she held on the better chance she had to live. The next morning I opened the door, thinking I might find her dead. Instead she raised her head just a little when she saw me. I got down on one knee and smoothed her tangled hair from her face, and her tail moved back and forth ever so slightly. She looked like she knew we were helping her. I picked her up and tucked her under my arm as I drove back to the clinic. At the clinic she received IV fluids and antibiotics over the next several days and little by little she improved. I began to think she was going to live.

I called Mrs. Cramer and said, "I want you to come over to the clinic."

She responded, "I'll be right over."

When Tracy came and told me she was there, I went to the kennel and opened Olive's cage door.

Olive still looked weak and mighty scraggly but when I said to her, "Mama's here to get you!" I think she knew by the tone of my voice what I meant.

Her tail moved just a little more than the night of the operation. I put her under my arm and off we went to see mama. We came through the door and Mrs. Cramer saw her for the first time since the surgery. Her face brightened and she said, "I can't believe it! She's alive! I'm so happy--this is like a miracle."

Doc, could you put me to sleep, too?

Some things in practice are very serious and I think this was the most sobering for me. It was a hot August afternoon, and it was warmer than usual inside the clinic because our air conditioner could not keep up with the constant opening and closing of the front door.

Tracy came into the office and said, "Mr. Brady is in the exam room with his dog to be put to sleep, and he can't talk, because of his throat surgery, so you will have to write notes back and forth. I put a notepad out on the table for you."

Mr. Brady had been forced to give up his accounting firm when he was diagnosed with throat cancer nine months earlier. Eighteen years ago he had picked up Buddy, a small mixed breed dog, from the animal shelter as a very young puppy. Mr. Brady had been coming in with Buddy ever since and he had the best care and love any dog could ever have. They were inseparable.

I had asked him many years ago, "How did you pick out Buddy with all the dogs at the shelter to choose from?"

He told me, "When I went to the shelter there must have been a hundred dogs to choose from. The particular cage that he was in had four dogs, all of them in the five to fifteen pound range. His three cage mates came to the front of the cage, wagging tails and barking, but Buddy stayed at the back lying down. He looked up at me, over the heads of the others, as if to say, '*I know you won't pick me so I won't waste the effort to get up.*' There was something about his sad eyes that I was drawn to. I went on down the line of cages and I looked at the others in a methodical fashion but I couldn't get those eyes out of my head. I had to have him."

Going into the room I saw that Mr. Brady was standing at the exam table with his sister by his side. Buddy, now a very old dog, and very sick, was on the table. Buddy's brown hair was a mess. Missing in spots, dried out and crusty. At 16 years old he didn't move much on the table. The average life span of all dogs is about 12 years. At his prime he weighed 15 pounds, but now he looked gaunt at only 11 pounds.

The discomfort on Mr. Brady's face was evident. He was only in his 50s and had sandy blonde hair and a white shirt that looked like a hospital gown. He looked much older than his years. He was thin with pale drawn skin, and he began writing on the pad Tracy had laid out for us, "Buddy has been very sick throwing up after every meal and now he won't eat at all."

After I read the note I looked at him and said I would examine him now. I checked him over, knowing in my mind that there was nothing left that I could do for Buddy, but I wanted Mr. Brady to see that I wasn't rushing to declare him untreatable. He was in the complete end stage of kidney failure.

My back was to Mr. Brady as I washed my hands in the sink, giving me a little time to compose myself for what I had to say to him. This part of being a veterinarian is the hardest.

Turning back to the table, I said, "There is nothing more that can be done, and the best thing is to let Buddy go. We need to put him to sleep so he won't have to suffer any more."

As he took in what I said the tremendous anguish he felt was evident. His face contorted. He was thinking of his best friend in the world.

It was several minutes before he picked up the pen and wrote something on the pad, "I think you are right. The way he's been suffering--it's time. I know it's the right thing to do."

I explained to him how it's done.

"We give Buddy an overdose of anesthesia in the vein and he goes to sleep and sleeps forever. It's painless and takes only five seconds to work."

Mr. Brady nodded gravely. I went to the back, got my syringe and vial of anesthesia, and then came back into the room. We gently shaved Buddy's front leg to prepare to give him the injection.

Mr. Brady's face was twisted with pain. As I began to wipe down his leg with alcohol he began to write something on the pad. I paused to wait for the note. When he had finished I began to read what it said.

It said, "Doc, could you put me to sleep, too?"

I felt like crying, as I knew he meant it that he did not have long to live himself. I shook my head to say no. I injected the anesthesia into Buddy's vein in his leg and he went to sleep peacefully. Mr. Brady sobbed and bent over Buddy and held him tight.

This was one of the most gut-wrenching and profound experiences in my life.

Chart Codes

My children, Rob and Suzy, were often at my clinic, as was my wife, Dee, who served as our bookkeeper. It was a family business, after all, and as the kids grew, so did their involvement at our office. During the summer months of their adolescence, Rob and Suzy sometimes worked part-time at our clinic. They would help walk dogs in the back, clean kennels and sometimes help with office filing.

The summer when Suzy was 14, I tasked her with going through several large file cabinets to see which records had not been updated in years and which could be discarded. She set to work on this project, going one by one through the client charts. After several hours, she came to ask me what all the codes handwritten at the top of the charts meant.

"Nearly every chart has a note at the top, Dad," she observed. "What does PIA mean?"

Tracy, our office manager, chuckled as she passed by and quickly walked away. Sadly, I had to explain that PIA meant "pain in @$!" Fortunately, Suzy observed that this was only indicated on a few cards. She also noticed that more than half of all the client cards indicated a percentage discount at the top.

"Dad, do you know that more than half of your clients get a 10, 20 or 30 percent discount?"

I hadn't realized that it was nearly this many, but I had to trust her finding. She also saw that almost all of the cards included little notes about the client or pet.

Played Little League with Rob

Church

Girl Scouts with Suzy

Son a freshman at Univ. of Florida

Mother-in-law's neighbor

Suzy was tickled by all these comments, but they were very helpful to me in all my years of practice. I learned over the years that it was important to remember people's names and a little something about their lives. I saw my mentor Alan, from my first days as a veterinary intern in Plant City, use this trick. He taught me that it's very important to remember people's children, animals and details about who they are. It made practice fun.

Goblin — Being Cavalier

When animals are unruly, bite or scratch we wrote BITES on the upper right corner of the medical chart, just as we indicated many other little notes about the pet or client. This information was helpful in preparing for what you might find in the exam room.

During one visit from a client, I read the chart for Goblin, a 12-pound black male cat.

BITES was clearly written in the proper spot.

Upon entering the exam room, I greeted Mr. and Mrs. Cornett and Goblin, who they had taken out of his carrier and was hissing at me as we talked. Paula, our animal technician, brought in a blanket and we proceeded to wrap Goblin up in it like a burrito. This was a standard procedure for handling fractious cats.

I said to the Cornetts, "We are going to take Goblin to the back to give him his vaccinations."

Up on the table in the back I gave him his vaccines under the skin by the shoulder area and he did not struggle at all. I reached inside and wrapped my hand around his body as he lay there quietly and gently lifted him out of the blanket. I was now thinking how I was *Mister Super Vet,* and I decided that I would be cavalier and carry him back under my arm to his waiting parents only 15 feet away.

Well, I picked him up with no blanket around him and headed out. So far so good! I wasn't more than three steps when he exploded and raked both of my arms with his claws in about a half second. As I was getting raked I began to RUN to the exam room to get him back to his parents. By the time I was putting him back on the table both of my arms were dripping with blood.

I have to learn things the hard way.

Now when I'm talking to someone with a new puppy and they are worried that he might hurt the cat who has been a resident in the house for several years I tell them the cat's front end is like a meat grinder when provoked. Don't worry about the cat!

Won't Stop Bleeding

It seems like whenever taking care of an animal of a close friend or family member, whatever can go wrong will go wrong.

Bob Evers was my electrician and had done the wiring on a building I had built. He was sure a nice guy with a friendly smile. I had gotten to know Bob fairly well through our business relations. During construction of the building he would drive out with his dog and check on his men's work. Every place Bob went Sandy, his golden retriever, was right there on the front seat beside him. She was the best dog. When he got out of the truck she always went with him into the buildings under construction. She was never on a leash but always stayed close by while Bob did his work. Needless to say, Sandy had the life all dogs dream of, going everywhere with her master every day.

Bob and I became close friends over the years.

When the day came for Sandy's spay operation, Bob brought her into the clinic on an empty stomach as was standard procedure.

He asked "Joe, when will she be ready to go home?"

I replied, "I'll operate on her this morning and after she wakes up from the anesthesia she'll be able to go home this afternoon."

After checking that Sandy was ready for her surgery I asked Paula, my veterinary nurse, to bring her to the surgery room. Drawing the appropriate amount of anesthesia into a syringe I gave it to her in the vein in her front leg. She went to sleep immediately and as her mouth was held open I inserted an endotracheal tube down her throat. Then we hooked the gas machine to the tube and began to administer the anesthesia.

Scrubbing up and donning my surgical gloves, cap and mask, I began the operation that I had performed thousands of times before. The surgery was routine with no extra bleeding.

Several hours later Paula told me that when she had checked Sandy, she was bleeding badly. We took her out of her cage and on the exam table observed that blood was leaking from her incision site. The color in her gums was nice and pink and she was active and alert so I put a tight body bandage around her stomach. Sometimes after surgery the little capillaries, tiny arteries and veins on edge of the incision, will for some reason bleed more than usual and this tight bandage is usually all that's needed.

About an hour later, when I was checking on her, there was a large amount of blood coming out around the bandage.

I called Bob and said, "Sandy is bleeding after her surgery and I can't stop it with a bandage. I'm going to have to go back inside her and see if she has popped a suture inside."

As a surgeon these are the things that give you grey hair. Every animal is different and when excessive bleeding occurs the first thought is maybe I missed a bleeder.

I put Sandy back on the surgery table and went through the same anesthesia routine. I opened her up by removing my original sutures and looked inside the abdomen to find the source of the bleeding. There was a lot of blood, which I sopped up with gauze sponges, and proceeded to look closely at each of the three suture knots I had placed on the two ovaries and uterus. None of these areas were leaking blood as I had feared. Also, no other area in the abdomen was bleeding. I was perplexed. Finding no bleeding and nothing to repair, I sutured her back up again and thought about a blood clotting problem.

We did a clotting time test on her blood and found that it took over eight minutes for her blood to clot. Normal clotting time is three minutes.

I called Dr. Goldson, a specialist, and together we tried to figure out what was happening with Sandy. We made a list of possible causes, and rat poison was at the top of the list. This was good because it was a problem with a possible solution. Rat poison (coumadin) is a powerful anticoagulant, or blood thinner.

I called Bob and said, "I just finished going back in her abdomen and can't find any bleeders that would cause this problem. Do you know of any way Sandy could have gotten into rat poison?"

After a pause he replied, "Now that you say that we have had a problem with rats in our shop, so we put out bait. Sandy has the run of the shop most of the time."

Bingo--I thought to myself!

I replied to Bob, "I may have the cause of her problem and a way to cure her if I can keep her alive long enough."

We checked her blood count and determined that she didn't need a blood transfusion. The plan was to wrap her abdomen tightly again and start her on the antidote for rat poison which is vitamin K.

I called Bob, "The rat poison is the cause of her bleeding and we're starting the antidote." He replied, "I'm glad you found the cause--we should have never put that stuff out."

Over the next few days Sandy steadily improved.

I called Bob and said, "I think she's well enough to go home now."

He was elated.

"I've missed her terribly. It's been mighty lonely riding without her," he replied.

It was a joyous event for us when he came in to get her. She ran out the door when she saw him, kissed him on his cheek and just about wrung her tail off wagging it so much!

Sandy lived to be a ripe old age and was never that sick again.

Profound Eye-Opening

Being a veterinarian in a busy practice, I wouldn't normally visit the dog pound on my time off. It was sort of like a bus driver riding the bus on his day off. I hadn't been to the pound for at least ten years. However, a new pound had been built recently and all the veterinarians were invited to come in the evening to see the new facility. I drove out there after work Thursday.

The new building was all concrete and located in an industrial area of town. I got there a little late. A friend of mine, Dr. Jim Hughes, came in about the same time. All of the other veterinarians had already been given a tour, so an animal technician took Jim and me on a tour of the new place. He showed us the new and modern floors, equipment, cages, etc. It was all very nice but I wasn't prepared for the last room on that tour.

The last room, about 20 feet by 30 feet, had a walkway down the middle with animal cages lining both sides. Each cage held two or three dogs. There was a total of about 75 animals. The dogs looked exactly like dogs we see every day in our practice--all sizes and colors. White with brown spots, solid black, floppy ears, erect ears, old, young. They jumped up on the gates and they looked happy.

Jim and I were down on one knee petting them and sticking our hands in the cages so they can lick our fingers when the fellow giving the tour said, "You know if we can't find a home for the dogs in this room by tomorrow, they will all have to be put to sleep to make room for more."

I felt awful as what he had said sunk in. It felt like I had been socked in my stomach. It was hard for me to imagine that all these beautiful dogs could be put to sleep. I'll never forget that night. From that night to this day when I'm asked by people *what kind of dog should we get,* I tell them to go out to the dog pound and take a walk around there first.

Cat in Fan Belt

The call came on a chilly March night at 11:45 pm (chilly in Florida is 50 degrees). Gene Rainy was on the line, "Doc, I started my car to leave for work and a cat is screaming under the hood of my car. Could you come right away? I don't know what to do."

I replied, "I'll be right there."

Outside cats love to get up in the motor of cars at night because the leftover heat from the engine is warmer than sleeping outside. I gathered everything I could think of that I needed, including a pair of side-cutting pliers that would cut a fan belt, and I drove over to the apartments where Gene lived. As I pulled into the parking lot he met me in a very agitated state.   "Right after I started my car, I heard all the commotion in the engine and immediately turned off the motor. I have been afraid to open the hood for fear of what I might find," he said.

We walked over to his car and he opened the hood. The parking lot was dark and it was hard for me to see where all the commotion was coming from. I could hear a struggling sound down towards the bottom of the motor. Not seeing anything from above, I got down under the front of the car and looked up into the motor. I could see a calico cat at the front of the motor. As my eyes began to adjust to the dim light I could see that her right hind leg was caught in the fan belt. I knew she was a female before I had even gotten up close to her in the semidarkness because all calico cats are female.

I went back to my car and I got out all the equipment that I had brought. The most urgent thing I had to do was get that fan belt cut. I worked from the top with my side cutters to try to get the belt cut. The belt had wire inside and I thought I'd never get it cut. This young cat was barely moving and quiet at this point, as shock had set in.

After the belt was cut, I was able to gently slide the kitty out. She looked up at me as if to say *thanks* with a worn-out expression. She looked to be about four months old. She was tired out, and I put her on the front seat of my car.

I said, "Gene, I'll take her back to the clinic with me."

He said, "It's not my cat, but I want to take care of her expenses."

He was a very caring person. I thought to myself that I would just charge for the barest expense I had incurred.

As I drove back to the clinic the kitten lay there quietly, looking up at me from time to time. Her leg was probably broken, but not bleeding. I could sense that she knew I was going to help her out of this terrible episode.

Although the leg was broken and badly damaged, I didn't have to amputate it. I put a pin in the leg to repair the fracture, and she recovered completely over the next few months. Gene decided to keep her because we couldn't locate any owner. He named her PL, which stood for parking lot from whence she came.

Antifreeze

Dogs and cats love the taste of antifreeze and it doesn't take much of it to kill them.

Ping was a Lhasa Apso/Jack Russell mix with chestnut brown hair except his feet and muzzle which were black. He weighed about 19 pounds, and with sunken dark eyes and rough haircoat he looked awfully sick.

Mr. Tanner, a quiet and respectful young man, placed him on the table and said, "He has been vomiting and not eating for the last two days. I'm really getting worried about him."

I could tell Ping felt awful. His skin was dry. A test on his urine showed crystals which confirmed that he had lapped up antifreeze. Antifreeze causes crystals to form in the kidneys and destroys them. Death soon comes if nothing is done. That green puddle you see under cars is antifreeze leaking from the radiators. It takes only one and a half teaspoonfuls to kill a cat and about two tablespoonfuls to kill a 10-pound dog. I wish they would put something bad-tasting in it so that animals would avoid drinking antifreeze, like the way they treat natural gas with a foul odor so that a leak can be detected.

Now back to business.

"Ping's got antifreeze poisoning and needs treatment fast," I said to Mr. Tanner.

The antidote for antifreeze is ethanol (ethyl alcohol) given intravenously. This of course is the star ingredient in beer, wine and liquor. I thought about where I would get pure ethanol. It's not something I stocked in my clinic. I called the local human hospital to see if they had any. They didn't. What could I to do now? I had read that grain alcohol sold in the liquor store could be used. I went down to the liquor store and bought a fifth of 190-proof grain alcohol.

When I got back to the clinic I began Ping's treatment with the grain alcohol given intravenously. Over the next few days Ping slowly recovered and soon went home. Mr. Tanner didn't have enough money to pay the entire amount so I only charged him what he could afford, which was less than a fourth of the bill. It was very rewarding for me to have played a part in saving Ping's life because so many animals poisoned with antifreeze don't live. This type of poisoning usually goes undiagnosed or the animal dies before treatment.

Duke and Tom

My son's dog Duke was a 55-pound Doberman Pincher with beautiful black shiny hair. His personality was magnificent. He was the nicest dog, and wouldn't hurt a fly. Even though he was a breed of dog from Germany, he sure wasn't cold hardy. He would get cold and shiver in the winter. Sometimes we'd put him in the laundry room at night with a blanket over him in the winter, and we lived in warm Florida.

He loved to play outside, but only if we went out there with him. Otherwise he would come to the back door and stand there till someone let him in.

Tom was my daughter's orange and white cat, and he was great.

One time we were watching television in our living room and my son said, "Look at this, Dad."

My son was laying on the floor beside an end table with the top drawer partially open. He put his hand up to the edge of this apparently empty drawer and wiggled his finger just above the top edge. All I could see was a paw come up over the edge and bat his finger. Tom was down in the drawer but out of sight. It was the funniest thing seeing them play that game.

One Sunday morning our whole family was sitting at the table having breakfast and looking out the window at the pool. Duke was by the edge of the pool with his head down and was backing up with Tom's entire head in his mouth. All that could be seen of Tom was his body from the neck down. He was upside down, feet pointed up, and being dragged backwards. He wasn't struggling or resisting.

We immediately jumped up from the table and ran out saying, "Duke, stop it! Bad boy!"

Duke opened his mouth and Tom jumped right up.

We picked up Tom and carried him into the garage where he liked to stay, while stroking his head and saying, "Good boy, Tom."

He wasn't hurt in any way.

We resumed our breakfast, and no more than 10 minutes had past, when we looked out the same window. To our surprise Tom was standing next to Duke, rubbing his head slowly up and down on Duke's front legs. I guess that's just the way they liked to play with each other. I sure wish I had a picture of Tom's head inside Duke's mouth.

Many people believe that dogs and cats cannot live

together peacefully in the same house, but in my professional and personal experience, this is not the case.

Conclusion

Looking back at nearly 50 years of veterinary practice, I have been blessed with a wonderful career and a wonderful life. It has been a stressful, satisfying, exhausting, exhilarating, and filled with moments that confounded me, surprised me, and taught me about many things. I have been surprised that even after all these years, it still hurts to put any animal to sleep, and it never stops hurting to see the client's grief in losing a beloved pet. I am convinced that life would be easier if our pets got to live as long as we humans do. I am also continually surprised by how different each animal and his or her personality is. Every one of them has a different personality. I have seen many pets of the same breed, of the same color and size, with very different demeanors. As an example, it is certainly true that not every pit bull is a fighter, and not every yorkie is a lover. They certainly can't be grouped by breed, size, color, etc.

I have seen many changes to veterinary medicine and practice over the course of my career. The scientific advances have been incredible. Many more animals have the chance to live now than when I first started. When I began we were limited to just X-rays for diagnosing internal complications and problems. A dog with a treatable heart valve problem would have been missed by this older technology, but now with CT scans, MRI, and sonogram technology, these problems can be discovered and treated effectively. Also, animal abuse is now a punishable crime, whereas back in the day such cruelty was often overlooked.

Many other things have changed, too. Sadly, at many veterinary schools the course of medical ethics has been dropped from the required curriculum. Ethics are rules of conduct that are above ordinary laws. For me, it has been more important to uphold my ethical principles than to sell products like unneeded shampoos or services like unnecessary surgery or tests. During my time a small practice was successful based upon the service to customers, in my case clients and their animals and how well I treated them. Today large corporations rule much more of the veterinary practice than many years ago. The bottom line for a business is making profit. The larger the business, the more important the profit becomes, often at the expense of the customers or clients. These large corporations ask veterinarians to compromise their ethics by recommending that so many EKGs be performed each month, or special shampoos or pet foods be recommended for purchase from the large corporation. It's no surprise that the same large corporation owns the dog food company and often the lab where the tests are performed.

Despite the changes, I would recommend choosing to become a veterinarian, if one has spent some time working at an animal clinic. I have heard some say that they would like to be a veterinarian because they love animals. However, this is just the start. An interest in science and living things is essential, as well. I remember well one young man who worked at our practice during his high school years. This young man was very bright and ambitious and had all the makings of a great veterinarian. However, in working at the clinic, he found that he could not endure it when animals needed to be put to sleep. His love of animals was so great that even ending their suffering was too difficult. He went on to become a successful airline pilot and later earned the rank of captain.

In reflecting on my practice, I am most proud that I was able to maintain my own ethical standards and give the best care that I could at the time. The rewarding moments far outnumber the disappointing times, and I would choose this career again even if I were starting it all over. Being a veterinarian has been good to me, for sure.

The fulfilling relationships with classmates, employees, clients and their pets have been a great benefit to my career. During the years our clinic was like one big family, and one that has brought me much joy. I am grateful also for the life our veterinary practice was able to provide to my family and me. Dee, Rob and Suzy were a big part of our practice over the years. Dee particularly was the best partner in life and in business that I could have ever asked for. I was fortunate that I felt comfortable with medicine, surgery and the care of animals. However, the general workings of any office, creating schedules, paying bills and taxes, ordering supplies and so much more, was something that my talented wife excelled in, and she lifted that burden from me. Some years ago my eldest grandson was visiting from his New England home and wanted to spend the day at work with me. I gave my eight-year-old grandson a lab coat, which swallowed him, and off we went in and out of exam rooms seeing clients and their animals. Although this same grandson is now a grown man, this moment is a great snapshot of the moments that I love during my practice.

    I have been very blessed and very fortunate to have experienced this beautiful veterinary life.

.

Acknowledgements

I would like to express my thanks to some extraordinary people who have helped me during my career as a veterinarian and as I wrote this memoir. It would be impossible to list all the special people in my life, but here is a start. Dr. James Robinson was my first mentor and gave me both my first job as a teenage vet technician, and as a rookie veterinarian. Auburn University's Dr. Patsy Tier was instrumental as a support and mentor while I was a vet school student.

In crafting this memoir, my daughter Suzy Priest Tkacik has provided tremendous support in editing and publishing this work. I would like to thank Dr. J.T. Vaughn, Dr. Maury Linkous and Chris Linkous for their contribution in proof-reading this work and the medical references. Jeanne DiPretoro and Allison Perry provided invaluable proof-reading help, as well. Jen Oseid created the lovely cover art, and Rudy Lopez captured the artful cover photo.

Finally, I would like express my deepest thanks to my family for all of their love and support throughout my life. My children, Rob and Suzy, have been the best kids I could hope for, and I am blessed to have seen my family grow with my son-in-law Michael Tkacik and my three grandsons Charlie, Ben and Samuel. My lovely wife Dee Priest has been my partner, my closest advisor and my right arm throughout the whole journey.

Made in the USA
Columbia, SC
03 July 2018